CONFESSIONS OF A PREACHER'S DAUGHTER

By Tameka Lovett

SELF HELP/INSPIRATIONAL
YOUNG ADULT/AFRICAN AMERICAN

ISBN-13: 978-1-944110-43-7

Edited by **Armani Valentino**

for College Boy Publishing

Published for print & digital distribution by **Armani Valentino**
Inside Designed & Setup by **Armani Valentino**

Cover Design by **Armani Valentino**

© 2019. Tameka Lovett. All Rights Reserved.

No part of this book may be reproduced or transmitted in any form or by any means, electronic or mechanical, including photocopying, recording, or by any information storage and retrieval system, without permission in writing from the publisher.

Published in Dallas, TX, by College Boy Publishing. College Boy Publishing is a division of The College Boy Company & ArmaniValentino.com.

Copies of this book may be ordered directly from www.collegeboypublishing.com. Please allow up to 7-10 Business Days for delivery.

The author is available for keynote addresses, workshops, panel discussions, consultations, and radio & television interviews by emailing collegeboypublishing@gmail.com

Printed in the United States of America

08 09 10 11 12 TLAV 5 4 3 2 1

CONFESSIONS OF A PREACHER'S DAUGHTER

Written by

Tameka Lovett

Dedicated to the Women who paved the way before us, those of us here, and those for whom we now pave the way.

Confessions of a Preacher's Daughter

1. The Mind of the Girl	1
2. Cherries & Guts	13
3. Babies and More Babies	19
4. The Next Step of Real Life	25
5. Trying to Find One's Self	33
6. The Decision	41
7. My Exposure	45
8. Lies & Shame	53
9. Persecution & Confusion	59
10. The Scent of a Man	69
11. Enough is Enough	75
12. The Tongue	89
13. Who are you judging?	95
14. Temptations	101
15. Help or No Help	107
16. What Does It Take?	111
17. Pressure	117
18. Trying to Overcome it All	121
Epilogue	133
Poems by Tameka	137
Prayer For You	152
Bibliography	153

INTRODUCTION

Hello, this is a journal of the many experiences I had to endure growing up. I share many parts of my life, from childhood to young adulthood, and therefore letting you into my mindset when making many decisions and the outcome of them. I hope to help other young girls and women who are in need of emotional healing from their past. You're not alone!

And the story begins....

I grew up in a small town in Arkansas. I am the oldest of my mother's children. My mom was 15 when she got pregnant with me; I never knew my biological father because he chose to stay out of my life. It wasn't until I was in my late 30's that he decided to be a part of my life. My mom was a quiet person, and she loved crafting and making clothes for others; she was one of the best seamstresses in town.

The only man I knew as father was my stepfather. He was pretty much the decision maker in the house, his way or no way. I was a very timid child, but I always seemed to get into trouble at school for some of the silliest things.

When I was in the 5th grade, my mom told me I couldn't go swimming with the rest of the 5th graders, but I decided I was going to go anyway. So I got on the bus to go, and when we got to the YWCA, I got into the pool in my t-shirt, bra, and panties. My coach was embarrassed.
He told me to put my clothes back on. When I got back to school, I was so wet that my teacher made me sit on top of the heating unit until my mom brought me some more clothes so I could change. My coach started calling me, The New Miss Sports Illustrated Swimsuit Cover Model," and my teacher laughed about this incident. To this day she has talked about me to all of her students.

For the most part, I was a meek child and was often overlooked in school. I had a C average throughout school, but I enjoyed reading books. I had a vast imagination and could tell some outrageous make-believe stories. I was always different from the other kids at school. I was constantly bullied and picked on, and no one really cared to play with me or be my friend. Even going into my teenage years, I began to think people didn't like me, although I had done nothing wrong to them. I didn't fit in with my other schoolmates, and I couldn't quite figure out why.

Tameka Lovett

CHAPTER ONE

THE MIND OF THE GIRL

CHAPTER ONE—The Mind of The Girl

January 1993

    I remember when Christmas Break was over I woke up one morning and was thinking to myself like, "Dang I got to go to school today." I was supposed to be going on a school field trip, but I had got in trouble a few days before because some kid told my mom I was on the school bus cursing. Also, a few days before my dad had been listening to my conversations on the phone, with my best friend while we talked to a boy on three-way calling. We weren't talking about anything that amounted to something, but to him, it was a big issue. I got off the phone, and he told me to put the phone up and to come into the kitchen. I did as I was told; he was standing there with an empty milk jug and asked me why was it left on the sink. I told him that I forgot to put it in the trash. My dad took off his belt and told me to hold my hand out. I held my hand out, and he slapped it with the belt. It hurt so bad that I jerked my hand back, but he just kept on swinging and ended up hitting my wrist and my shoulder. I screamed. "Ouch, you hit my wrist" Afterwards my mom came out of the bedroom to address my so-called cursing on the bus. I denied the cursing because I didn't remember doing it, but I didn't argue.

    The next morning as I was getting ready for school I looked at the blue and green bruise on my arm and thought, "I am so glad it's winter time so that this won't show at school. "I put the rest of my clothes on and walked to school. If my parents had found out that I had been walking to school instead of riding the bus sometimes, I would have gotten my butt whipped for that as well. The school was walking distance, and I liked to use the time to think in silence.

Confessions of a Preacher's Daughter

My mom was 19 when she got pregnant with me and married the man I now know as my dad. I had never met my biological father, so this man was my dad. I knew I had another dad out there because I could remember him showing up at my house and knocking on the door; my mom told me not to answer the door or look out the window. My biological father called once, and I answered the phone. I remember him saying, "Hello Tameka! This is your dad."

Before I could say anything, my mom took the phone from me. After that day, my mom didn't allow me to answer the phone anymore for a long time.
As adults, we seem to think that children don't or can't remember things because they were so young, but even though I was a young child between the ages of 3 and 8, I still remember a lot.

As a young girl, I was looked down on in grade school; all the other kids bullied and picked on me. I was always the different one, and I didn't understand why I was so different. I was always the last one picked for P.E. teams. I cried a lot at school because it seemed to me that no one wanted to be around me. I just wanted someone to play with or be my friend. I fell as if I didn't have a childhood because I was barely allowed to go anywhere. I could not participate in school activities, sleepover friend's house, attend their parties, or play in community organized sports. It wasn't until after my parents divorced and I was in high school that my mother allowed me to participate in school dances and other extracurricular activities.

At a very young age, I dealt with demonic forces. One night I was in bed and rolled over to a smiley face on the wall that started talking to me. I also remember waking up to a big snake leaning over me with its mouth

CHAPTER ONE—The Mind of The Girl

open. I would see images and wake up unable to move, open my eyes, or even scream for help. I would try to cry out to my mother, but she never came because there was no sound coming from my mouth. My mother would tell me I was just dreaming, but now I look back on those memories, and they are still here, so I know that it was no dream. I reflect on the many unusual things that happened to me as a child, and I realize that the devil was after me from the beginning.

The enemy had pursued my family for many generations, and so much has been passed down, but I have decreed and declared that it ends with me. See when you have a calling on your life, and God has a destined plan for you then the devil will try to destroy you before you have a chance to walk in it.

Stay alert! Watch out for your greatest enemy, the devil. He prowls around looking for someone to devour. (1st Peter 5:8 NLT)

I had always been afraid of the man who took me in as his own daughter. I would hide from him under my bed whenever my mom would leave me alone with him. It seemed like each time she left me, he would think of a reason to whip me. One time I hid from him so long he thought I had run off. When my mom got back home, I reappeared, but I still got beat for hiding and not coming out when he called my name.

The time came when he changed his life, gave it to God, and began preaching the Gospel of Christ. He pastored several different churches until he got tired of organized religion and then he decided to leave that denomination and be an independent ministry. His way of chastising a child, however, stayed the same. He would make me lie face down on

Confessions of a Preacher's Daughter

the floor and put my head up under a chair while he whipped me. I was a bright skinned girl, and bruises showed up quickly, so I would have to try and hide them from people. The things I got whippings for were well deserved, but I didn't feel some things were worthy of the severity of the punishment. My mom never believed me when I told her that my teachers would ask why I had bruises. Most of the time I stayed in my room sleeping or reading a book because I didn't want to be anywhere near my parents.

Fathers do not provoke your children to anger by the way you treat them. Rather bring them up with discipline and instruction that comes from the lord. (Ephesians 6:4 NLT)

One day during lunch, I told my cousin about things that she already knew and didn't know. I admitted I was going to run away from home in two days. She said it wasn't a good idea to just run away without having anywhere to go, and suggested I wait and she would let me know what she thought about it the next day. Towards the end of the day, my thoughts went back to what I was focusing on before school. I was thirteen with a 3-year-old brother that thought the world of me, but I was so focused on my own problems that I paid him no attention. I wondered if he would get the same beatings I got when he was older since he was our dad's biological child and I was not.

I got home from school that day at about 3:30 that day and my mom was in the kitchen. I spoke then went to my room; to my surprise, she was behind me. She told me that my dad was working late, I could eat dinner, and she was about to lie down, and I needed to keep an eye on my brother. I waited until she was asleep and then I called my

CHAPTER ONE—The Mind of The Girl

cousin. She said she told her mom and grandfather why I was trying to get away from home, and I could stay with them. I told her I was going to walk to her house that night after my parents went to sleep.

It was freezing that night, and I had to walk about 3 miles to her house. I wrote my mother a note, telling her that I was running away because I was tired of the beatings and felt I was not being treated right. I also explained that I didn't want to live there anymore. I left the note on the kitchen counter and walked out the front door.

I was 13 years old and not the least bit afraid to run away, but I was fearful of being seen by the police, so dodged all the cars I saw. When I got to my aunt's house, I was freezing.

"What took you so long girl!" she said.

I responded with, "Do you realize how far I had to walk? It took me an hour to get here."

It was about 1:45 when I laid down on the couch; I thought about what my mom would feel when she saw the note and realized that I was gone.

I was awakened by my cousin's mom telling us to get to the bus stop for school. I didn't want to go because I knew my mom would come to school looking for me. I got through my 4th-period class, but then I got called to the counselor's office. She questioned me about why I had left my parent's house in the middle of the night. I just sat there for a minute thinking about how to answer her question. I finally let her know I was not happy at home and I felt like I was being abused. She looked at me for a split second then told me my aunt called the school and let her know that I had run away;

Confessions of a Preacher's Daughter

she felt that the school should know. She also told me that my mom came to the school shortly after my aunt called, but she only left a note telling me to return home that evening. My counselor talked to me some more and then sent me back to class.

When the day was over, I got on the bus with my cousin, and I told her that I was afraid of what was going to happen next. When we got back to her house, her grandfather sat down and told me that I could stay if I wanted and that he was going to do something to help me. As soon as we sat down to eat there was a knock on the door that sent chills up my spine. It was my mom, and she demanded that my cousin's grandmother open the door. They had some words, and then I heard my mom call my name and say, "Tameka you better come out this door right now." My cousin's grandma told her that I wasn't going anywhere, but I got up anyway and went to get my stuff. I told my cousin thanks for trying as I walked out the door.

Before we went home, my mom took me to visit a reform school and threatened to leave me. When we arrived and sat down, the guy in charge for that night sat down with us to discuss with me and my mom why I had run away. The man talked to me like I had just made up another one of my wild stories. I sat there listening to him tell me that I should not make up lies about my parents because they worked hard to take care of me. I was furious with my mom for bringing me to this place. When we got home, she told me that I was not going to get a whipping, but she grounded me for lying on my dad. I stared at the back of her head and thought to myself, "Lying? I am not lying!" I got out the car and went in my room and stayed there the rest of the day and didn't leave out until around 9 o'clock. Later I went into the kitchen

CHAPTER ONE—The Mind of The Girl

to get something to drink and then went back to my room. I really didn't want to read a book, and I didn't have a TV to watch, so I just stared idly up at the ceiling.

Sunday seemed to come fast that weekend, and I didn't pay too much attention to my dad Sunday morning when he got up to preach. My mind was on running away again, but this time I was going to do it the right way. After church one of the members asked me if I wanted to stay with her for a while because my mom had told her about what happened. I was shocked because I didn't know she knew about what I had done. I wanted to say yes, but I didn't because I was too afraid to tell her the truth. After we left, I wanted to go back and tell her I changed my mind, but I just got in the truck and rested my head on the window. On the way home I had to keep moving my head off my brother's booster seat because he wouldn't leave me alone. The entire ride all I heard was, "TaGekia... TaGekia...," since he could not say Tameka. It was kind of funny, but when he called me that in public it would embarrass me. Things died down a few weeks later, but my feelings about not wanting to be there never changed. Things only got worse for me. I experienced many unforeseen mental issues, and that was a lot for a teenager to work through. I felt utterly alone and like no one cared to understand what I was going through mentally.

My dad had a gospel singing group that was always traveling or performing somewhere. I loved going to church, gospel concerts, and being in the presence of so many people singing and praising God. I would sometimes watch in awe at the people falling out and speaking in tongues. I wanted to feel what they were feeling.

Confessions of a Preacher's Daughter

One of the group members started molesting me around the age of 10. There were times when he would tell me I was pretty and hug on me. It went so far that he touched me and stuck his hands in my clothes, and he made me touch him. Even though I knew it was wrong, I liked the attention and the compliments he gave me. No one at home told me how pretty I was or looked at me like I was special, so I craved the attention. Also, since I wasn't getting any affection or love at home, I thought this was okay.

See, that's how young girls are when they grow up without the love and attention they should have from their father; they will begin to seek it from somewhere else. It usually carries over into adulthood, causing them to make all the wrong choices when dating. I knew it was wrong, but mentally I was lost. I felt my parents didn't care about me, so I let him continue to sweet talk and touch me. He never got the chance to rape me, but I know if he had ever gotten the chance, he would have. I didn't tell my parents about it until I was around 30 years old.

Many young girls are molested and raped by close relatives, friends of the family, and sometimes by their parents. Most take the experience and internalize it and never speak about it until years later. Sometimes this becomes a pattern in families, and many women who have been raped or molested as a child or teenager grows up and has daughters of her own who seem to suffer the same fate. Ladies if this has happened to you, you must take charge and control your destiny. Speak out against that lustful sexual spirit that plagues your family, because you have the power to stop Satan's plan to destroy the women in your family. Stop being silent about what happened to you as a child, because by you telling your story, you may prevent it from happening to your children.

CHAPTER ONE—The Mind of The Girl

Now, if you are a teenager who is being molested or raped by anyone, then please do not do as I did and keep it a secret. There are lots of people who can help you and your family. Tell your parents when or if this happens to you, and if your parent is the violator, then tell an aunt or uncle, someone in your church family, or anyone who will help you get out of that situation. Sometimes, the first thought that comes to a child's mind is that they don't want to get anyone in trouble, but things like this must be told. Over the years there have been cases where the molester or rapist murdered the child to prevent them from letting anyone know what happened. Protect yourself and anyone else from these predators and report what is happening or has happened to you.

As parents, we must give them the love that they need, especially when there is no father figure in the home. They will begin to seek love and attention in the wrong places at a young age, and it will continue into adulthood; as a result, they won't know how to love anyone or even how to receive love from anyone who truly loves them.

CHAPTER TWO

CHERRIES & GUTS

CHAPTER TWO—Cherries & Guts

August 13, 1994

    I was naive and had no idea what was in store for me. When we arrived, my cousin left us in the living room and went outside to talk to his cousin. I asked to use the bathroom, and he showed me where it was. As I closed the door, I noticed there was no lock on the door. I flushed the toilet, went to the sink, and washed my hands. The guy came into the bathroom and told me he just wanted to kiss me, so I let him. I was enjoying it until he tried to take my clothes off. I was scared and told him I had to leave. He blocked the door, and I gave in. I didn't like what he did, and it hurt. After about 15 minutes it was all over. I left his house. My cousin asked me what I was doing, and I told her nothing. She laughed at me and said, "You were screwing in there!" I denied it, and she finally left the subject alone. I felt like a slut. Of all the ways to lose my virginity, I lost it on the bathroom floor. I could have gotten pregnant. My mother was already preparing to have another baby in September. What was I thinking?

May 1995

    One day in mid-May, my family and I sat down to eat supper, and my little brother sat at his table to eat. My mom was extremely quiet. For some reason, my brother didn't want to eat his food, so he started whining and holding his food in his mouth. Suddenly, my dad snatched his belt off, swung it, and slapped my 4-year-old brother across his back a few times. To my surprise, my mom spoke up this time and yelled, "Don't hit him like that." He struck my brother that it slightly knocked him forward. My dad looked her with a shocked expression, got up from the table, and went into his

Confessions of a Preacher's Daughter

study. I looked at my mom, but she said nothing else while my brother sat at his table, crying. I felt so sorry for him because I knew he didn't understand why he was being hit. A few months passed. One day my mom came into my room to tell me she was leaving my dad. She told me she would explain why after she moved out of the house. I was told to pack some of my stuff and to hide it so it wouldn't look as if anything was wrong. The next day we packed our clothes and went to the motel to stay. Once we got settled in she told me she was tired of the kind of whoopings I was receiving, being a pastor's wife, and other things I wouldn't understand. Once he started beating my brother, she said it was all she could take.

As I lay in the bed later that night, I heard my mom talking on the phone with my dad. It sounded like she was getting upset. I couldn't believe what I was hearing; my mom was standing up to my father.

The next few months went by slowly. My mom got a decent job and we moved into a small 3-bedroom mobile home. Things were a lot more peaceful for me now, but I had something brewing up in me. I couldn't explain the feeling that was coming over me, so I just ignored it and went on.

We eventually moved into a bigger house, and I fell in love with it as soon as I walked in it. I enjoyed being at home and the freedom of being able to cook something to eat and watch TV whenever I wanted to do so. I even had a TV in my room. My little brother had his own room, and my baby sister slept in the room with my mom. This life was all new to me, and I loved every bit of it. Things changed a lot for me I didn't know what freedom was, and I was overjoyed at the thought of being away from my father. I didn't have to worry about getting beat across the back for forgetting to

CHAPTER TWO—Cherries & Guts

take out the trash or because of a bad grade on a test at school. Unfortunately, once I got a taste of this new freedom, it went to my head.

There was another incident with a grown man during this time frame. The school bus driver I had, had taken an interest in me and what made him look so bad was the fact that he was a preacher. I was always the first he picked up and the last he dropped off. At first, I liked the attention until he started telling me that he wanted to take me to bed. Once again, I started letting a man touch me and look at my body. However, this time I got scared and told my mom. She reported it, and he got fired.

CHAPTER THREE

BABIES & MORE BABIES

CHAPTER THREE—Babies & More Babies

1996

It was my junior year in high school, and I was ready to graduate. I wanted to go to Grambling State University but didn't know what I wanted to major in. My best friend and I had both said we were going there when we graduated high school. Since we were in ROTC, we could have got into the ROTC college program with a high rank. I was ready for it, but sometimes things in life don't go as we've planned. Boy, was I in for a rude awakening?

My mom got remarried, and my new stepdad seemed to be okay. He seemed to be little crazy in the head, but he was alright. I met this boy on the school bus who sat in the seat behind me. He never talked to me, but I would catch him staring at me on the bus. One morning he got on the bus, and his hand accidentally touched my head, well at least that's what he said. He asked me where I lived and what grade I was in. I was kind of shocked when he told me he was a freshman. He was cute and dark skinned. I liked dark-skinned boys because the bright skinned boys were what we called "pretty boys." We talked for a few months on the phone and at school. Everyone would pick at me because he was a freshman and I was a junior, but I didn't care.

It was almost time for Homecoming and the person I wanted to ask ended up asking out my best friend. She asked me if I would be mad at her if she went with him. I told her it was cool, I mean, it wasn't like the guy was my boyfriend. I decided to ask the guy on my bus, and he said, "Yes." I had a good time with him at the dance. The next day he rode his bike to my house to see me. When he was ready to leave, I walked him to the end of the street. Then, he kissed me. Right in the middle of our kiss, I heard my mom screaming at me from her car. I just stood there for a minute. She told me to go back to the house. I was glad that she was on her way to work so I wouldn't have to listen to her speech.

My stepdad was on the phone all night that night. He had gotten to where he would keep the phone in the room with him all the time, now. The thought crossed my mind that he was cheating on my mom, but then I didn't think any more about it until a few weeks later. I was on the phone with my best friend around 11 o'clock, and someone beeped in. It was a woman asking to speak to him. I went to their bedroom and called his name a couple of times, but he didn't answer me. So, I told the lady that he was asleep and wouldn't get up. The next evening, he was hollering at my mom saying that his boss called and asked to speak to him, but I told the man no one with that name lived here. I tried to tell my mom what happened, but she accused me of lying and informed me that my step-dad was telling the truth. He was beginning to show his true self. I had already seen something was not right with him when they first got married.

There was this one night I was going to try and sneak my boyfriend in the house. Well, the neighbor's dog started barking, and my stepdad went outside and caught my friend behind the storage building. He came back in the house with my friend by his collar yelling, "Look what I found behind the storage building." My mom got mad at me and gave me the lecture about getting pregnant, and then she told me that she would be having another baby in February.

The rest of the school year went by fast. Before I knew it, it was summer break. I would be a senior next school term, and I couldn't wait. My guy friend and I started hanging out a whole lot, and soon you didn't see one without the other. We even began to sneak and skip school together. There were times when we were supposed to be at bible

CHAPTER THREE—Babies & More Babies

study or choir practice, but I would leave and go off somewhere with him and then come back to church. My pastor's wife caught us leaving the church one night, and she told on us.

December 1997

So far, my senior year had been going well. I was getting close to exam time, and the school had an open campus. My guy friend and I, and his cousin and his girlfriend went back to his mom's house until school hours were over. As we were walking, a girl that stayed around the corner from him was watching us, like she was jealous, but I didn't think too much about it.

I was going out my mind at the time because I hadn't had a period since November, so I hid my pads in my drawers and closet so that my mom won't find them unused. It had gotten so bad that when she cooked, just the smell of the food made me sick to my stomach. I told my best friend that I was pregnant, she couldn't believe it. I hadn't told anyone else how bad I felt. Here I was talking about going to Grambling State University and was going to be having a baby in September possibly. I knew my mom was going to flip when she found out because she was about to have another baby and I went and got pregnant. I hid my pregnancy from my mom, even after she had my baby sister in February; I still didn't tell her I was pregnant.

One night in the middle of March she woke me up about 1:00 am, and asked me why I had three (3) bags of unused sanitary pads in my closet. The question caught me off guard, and I told her I didn't know. She took out a pregnancy test and made me take it right then. The little plus sign took no time in coming up. She started fussing and told me to go back to bed. As she walked to her room, she was saying,

Confessions of a Preacher's Daughter

"Here I thought I had a virgin." I heard her on the phone with my boyfriend's mom soon afterward. The next day I stayed in my room until my mom went to work and my stepdad was gone. I called my boyfriend to see how he was doing. He said that his mom beat the mess out of him and told him he couldn't see me anymore, and that was final. Then, he told me he had been seeing another girl that was his age. His mom said it was alright for him to date her, but not me.

Not too long after my mom had the baby, she put my stepdad out. She never said why or anything, but he was gone. This left me pregnant with my brother and sisters to watch while my mom went to work. The next few months went by fast, and I was excited about graduation. I would finally be out of high school, which meant no more getting up early. I was not showing too much by the time May came around, and some people still didn't know I was pregnant. I was glad I wasn't showing. I had a few other classmates who were pregnant or had already had babies, so I didn't feel so bad about being pregnant.

CHAPTER FOUR

THE NEXT STEP OF REAL LIFE

CHAPTER THREE—Babies & More Babies

Graduation 1998
    The school year was almost over, and it was time for prom and the Senior All Night party. These last few days of school were always the most memorable for me and the most heartbreaking. I connected myself mentally and sexually with a guy I had been secretly head over heels for, and at the time, I didn't know what a soul tie was. It wasn't until later on in my adult years I found out when I had to face this person again. For almost four years I developed an obsession with this guy. He had a girlfriend, and I had a boyfriend, but I still wanted him.
    See, I had given my heart to a guy who wasn't even mine, and I became so emotionally attached to the guy that I didn't realize what the enemy was doing. We ended up sleeping together several times, and it messed my head up. He wasn't predestined to be my husband, and all through my adult years, I couldn't get this young man out of my mind. The feelings went away until I had to face him, and I had no other choice to tell him how I felt. When I finally released it, I could let it go after some months.
    That goes to show you how we can let the enemy hold us back from who God has for us, by causing us to give ourselves to men who are not for us. Years later, they're married and not even thinking about us, but we still can't seem to figure out why we can't find love. It's because we're bound to them through a soul tie we made, and we are still connected to that person. As young women and teenage girls, we must keep ourselves until God puts the right man in our lives. A soul tie can cause a lot of self-inflicted pain later down the line. We'll often find ourselves wondering why we can't go on or why we can't love anyone. You must break the soul tie before you can truly move forward.

Confessions of a Preacher's Daughter

Graduation is the day that we will all never forget. We had been outside in the hot sun all day practicing for graduation later that evening. By the time 7:00 pm came around I was exhausted. Just when it was time for us to line up to walk out on the field, I started feeling nauseous. I had to leave the line to go throw up behind a tree. I felt so bad, and I prayed that I could make it through the ceremony without getting sick again.

As the principal called my name, I heard family and family cheering for me from the stands. I walked onto the football field I started feeling faint headed, I said to myself, "Lord, please don't let me get sick right now." When I got back to my seat and put my head down, I felt better. Before I knew it, the principal was saying good luck to the class of 1998. We all stood up, threw our hats in the air, and cheered. We all hugged and cried as we got ready to go home. As I looked around at my classmates and I wondered what would become of them all. Then, I looked down at my belly and said, "Well, this is my next project. I am just ready for this baby to come on out."

Labor Day 1998

As I was sitting in church, I kept feeling a pain in my belly, but I didn't think much of it because I had been having the pain all week. I was starving after church, so I went back to my boyfriend's house and ate three chili cheese dogs. While I was there my water suddenly broke. I didn't know what it was supposed to feel like, but when I stood up water started running down my legs. His mom took me to the hospital around 2:30 pm. I was alright until I started throwing up all the junk food I had eaten earlier that day. My contractions started to hurt badly around 7:45 pm. By 9:30 pm I was

CHAPTER FOUR—Babies & More Babies

ready to have my baby. Minutes later I gave birth to a baby girl. I was so tired that I passed out from laboring and all the pain medicine the nurses had given me. However, I didn't stay asleep long. I woke up around 2 o'clock in the morning feeling energized. I got up and thought about the road ahead of me. Having a baby of my own was going to be fun to me; I had someone who would love me back. I didn't have to seek love from anyone else, and I didn't have to wonder if anyone in the world loved me.

My life at home with my baby and my little brother and sisters was very hard for me. My mom was working to support us, so that left me there to take care of my siblings. I didn't want to listen to my mom when she told me to do things. I thought I was grown and that my mom wasn't going to tell me anything. I became very rebellious, and I would have my male friends over when she went to work. My baby's dad had started seeing someone else while dating me at the same time.

I became so upset that I wanted to take my own life. I had never experienced someone hurting me like that, so I began to go into a deep depression. I hated my mom, and I felt like she hated me. I started to hate the way things were going in my life. I secretly began to throw fits, break stuff, and tear my room apart. I thought I was losing my mind, so I tried to end my life by taking a whole bottle of aspirin. Well, it didn't work. The only thing it did was make me sleep for a long time. I was feeling many emotions I didn't understand. I let hate build up in my heart against my mom. I felt like she was wrong for allowing my childhood to be taken away from me, for allowing my dad to beat me and verbally abuse me, and for not standing up for me as a young girl.

Confessions of a Preacher's Daughter

I even blamed her for my lack of knowing my biological father and for not letting him see me when he would come around. Most of my childhood was spent shut up in my room with no TV, and being shut off mentally from the outside world. I vowed that I would never treat my kids the way I was treated and steal their childhood from them.

By this time, my mom had let her husband come back. I think she felt it would all be better this time around, but things only got worse. I knew things that he was doing outside the house, but I never told my mom because at the time she wouldn't have believed me.

One of my cousins moved in with us, and it seemed as if my mom was treating her like the daughter instead of me. My mom would let her drive the car whenever she wanted, without a driver's license. I really couldn't be upset because, by this time, I had gotten into some trouble with the law for driving other people vehicles without a license and no proof of insurance. I had to get around the best way I could, so whoever would ever let me use their car I would use it. After my cousin moved in, I started going up against my mom more than ever before. I would argue with her in front of company and talk to her any kind of way. One day she finally told me I had to move out, so I stayed with one of my cousins. A few months later she let me come back home.

One day, after moving back home, the house caught fire. The fire started because I left a ragged mop and some chemicals that I had used to mop the floor too close to the water heater. The chemical reaction caused an explosion. The neighbors say they heard it from next door. The fire chief told us it was good we were not at home because no one would have survived.

CHAPTER FOUR—Babies & More Babies

My mom found somewhere else to stay after the incident, and I ended up having to get a job. I would walk from home to the babysitter's and then work every day. Little did I know, the road ahead of me was going to be full of more tests and attacks from the enemy.

CHAPTER FIVE

TRYING TO FIND ONE'S SELF

CHAPTER FIVE—Trying to Find One's Self

Well, the year 2000 had finally come. The past few years I had bounced from friend's and family's homes for quite a while because living arrangements never worked out. During this time, friends introduced me to weed and alcohol. I had jobs here and there, but I never kept one long because I didn't have a car to get to work. So, I spent my days drinking and getting high. It felt good, and I liked the feeling it gave me. During this time in my life, I let my daughter go and live with her father and grandmother in Georgia for a year because I was struggling to make it on my own in the world. Letting her go there was not a good idea, because instead of helping myself while she was away, I started smoking weed and drinking all the time.

One time, the guy I was dating had come to my house, and on this night after we had smoked, I began to laugh uncontrollably. After I went back into the house, I started to see black shadows and hear sounds I had never heard before. I felt so terrible that I was afraid I was about to die. My heart was beating so fast I thought it was going to come out of my chest. On top of that, I could hear it just like someone was talking to me in my ear. "Yeah, I was really tripping."

After my experience with that, I said I wasn't smoking anymore, and I would stick to drinking. I took a particular interest in men who were married or had a live-in girlfriend. I didn't care about what they had going on; I just wanted their attention. So, I sought out to get what I wanted. I was very conniving and sneaky. I got involved in an awful relationship and this one I brought all on myself. I was living with a guy I was dating, but we lived with his sister and her boyfriend. Well, her boyfriend started checking me out, and I liked it, so I decided that I was going to take what I wanted.

Confessions of a Preacher's Daughter

See I was bold, and even then, God was trying to get my attention, but I ignored him. I always knew how to read people and figure them out, so I could manipulate them well. God gives some of us the discernment of the spirits, and we don't even realize it. So, all these years I didn't know what all that was because my father as a minister never taught about things like that. Sometimes I thought I was crazy when I would tell people a certain situation would happen if they did this or that and it ended up happening. As far as I can remember, there weren't too many times I was wrong. I could also look at people and know what kind of person they were. I didn't understand the gift I possessed. There was a time when we were all riding, and the guy driving was speeding down the ice-covered road. I had my 4-year-old daughter in the middle seat, and the Holy Spirit said to me, "Pick your daughter up and put her in the floor in front of you." No sooner than I did that we slammed into the back of a car in the middle of the road. If I had left her sitting where she was, she would have gone flying through the windshield. God's hand was upon me even then.

So, the guy I was dating found out that I was sleeping with his sister's man. Yes, he jumped on me, but he and his sister got put out. So, I thought I was terrible because I had taken someone else's man and then got them evicted. She came back to the house a few times, and she could have killed me then, but she never bothered me. God whipped me for what I'd done because about a month later this man's house went up in flames for no apparent reason. So, that left us to live at a motel, and it wasn't the best one in town either. I decided it was time for me to get a job and stop goofing around, so I went and took classes to get my Certified Nurse's Aide License.

CHAPTER FIVE—Trying to Find One's Self

We found a one bedroom apartment, and that's when I found out what type of man he was. He began to drink all the time, come in late, and even tried to force me to marry him. Well that's one thing I knew was I wasn't dealing with, so I put him out.

He came back to get his things, and this night he was drunk, he forced himself on me, and while raping me, he was beating me in the head with his fist and choking me at the same time. After he climaxed, he got up and gathered his belongings and left.

I thought he was gone for good, but he came back a few days later. I was in my room getting ready for bed, and I saw his shadow at my window. I instantly knew he was coming to kill me, so I took off running out my front door and down the street. It wasn't my first time running down that street, because he had me running many times before. The neighbors would see me running and call the police on him. This night I was so afraid that I ran, turned a few corners, and hid in someone's shed until daylight struck. The sad thing about it was that I saw him when he left my apartment, he was walking at a fast pace while stuffing what I saw to be a small handgun into his coat pocket. When daylight emerged, I went around to a friend's house and told her about what had happened. I knew then it was God who had told me to run because this man was coming to put an end my life that night.

I was uneasy for the next couple of weeks. I had a new friend who seemed concerned about my safety, and he asked me if I wanted to move in with him and his mom. I thought about it for a few days, and I came to the decision that I would go ahead and move in with them to get away from my insane ex-boyfriend. I decided to get my daughter back at this time as well.

I moved in, and it was alright at first, but I was quickly drawn back into drinking and smoking weed again because my friend also smoked marijuana. Two months had passed, and he changed from the nice guy I had initially met. He would stay gone for long periods of time and blame it on the type of job he had.

The day came for me to see the light. It was Mother's Day morning, and he had stayed out all night. He came home that morning with red marks all over him. When I confronted him, he got loud with me and then stormed out the front door. I became so enraged I jumped in my car and chased him all the way out to the highway that was not too far away from where we lived.

The holy spirit rebuked me right there and reminded me of the particular road I was on, was the same road that many people including a cousin of mine had tragic wrecks on because of the dangerous curves and the narrowness of the road, so I turned around and went back to the apartment. The next day I got a visit from the woman he had been sleeping around with, and to my surprise, it was a woman I knew as a young girl from church. She was about 20 years older than us. She told me he was her's and that I should go on about my business. So, I packed my stuff and went to live with a cousin of mine. Not too long after I moved in with her, I found out I was pregnant.

The next seven months were hard for me. I stayed stressed out because I was still hung up over my baby's dad. Until the day he came to my cousin's house in broad daylight with a loaded gun and called for me to come outside. I went to the car, and he was sitting in the car with a gun on the passenger's seat. He began to tell me how he was tired of every-

CHAPTER FIVE—Trying to Find One's Self

thing and felt like he was losing his mind. The whole time I was standing there I felt in my gut that was going to kill me. He picked the gun up and cocked it and put in his mouth. I knew then that there was something seriously wrong going on with him. Then he looked at me as if he wanted to shoot me, but he drove off. After this I would see him stalking me, he had me so afraid that I would have a police friend of mine follow me home at night when I would get off work.

When I was in the middle of my seventh month of pregnancy, a friend of mine and I had a bad car wreck. It totaled my car. To this day, I know it was God who spared our lives that evening. The truck hit me on the passenger side where the gas tank was. There was gas everywhere, and the car looked like someone had balled it up in their hands. My friend was ok, and since I was pregnant, they took me to the ER. I was released and sent home the same day.

A few weeks later I went into premature labor, which only lasted about 3 hours. I had a 3-pound baby girl, but she was not breathing when I had her, so the nurses rushed out of the room with her. I didn't even get a chance to look at her. The nurses took me back to my room, and about 45 minutes later they came in and took me to see my baby. She was so little; I had never seen a baby that small. I said then she must have been destined to be here and made the decision to change the name I had initially decided for her.

Later, that day I started having pains in my chest that traveled to my head, and soon my whole body was hurting. I told the nurses several times how I was feeling, but they only said it was heartburn and the after-effects of premature birth. "See the devil will use anyone to try and take you out." I began to go in and out of consciousness, and my body felt like it was about to explode. I knew I was on my deathbed and I was hurting so bad that I was ready to die. They brought my dinner tray into my room. I was in so much pain that I couldn't even sit up to look. The nurses never checked me to see where the pain was coming from nor did they do their routine blood pressure checks on me.

Now here is where God stepped in when the nurses left me for dead. I woke up at about 3 a.m. feeling fine. I wasn't hurting, and I had a burst of energy. I was a little thirsty, so I called for the nurse, and she came in with some pills; she told me they were my prenatal vitamins, blood pressure, and seizure medicine. I looked at her like she was crazy and told her that this was not my medication. She then exited the room and came back to let me know my blood pressure had started elevating and they couldn't get it to go down. She also informed me that at one point I started having seizures and that I possibly had a light stroke. I didn't remember anything after 5 o'clock that evening up until then. Tell me that wasn't God. Now I felt like nothing was wrong with me and was so close to death just hours ago, that it was unbelievable."

I was still to spiritually blind to see that God was sparing my life once again. I went home the next two days, but my baby had to stay because she was still too little. My newborn baby remained in the hospital for about 2 ½ weeks. She endured a lot as a baby. She had surgery on her eye at the age of 2 months in which the doctors told me she would still probably lose vision in that eye. They diagnosed her with a rare nervous disorder which would cause developmental delays and severe learning disorders. When she turned three years old, she started having seizures and spent many days in and out the hospitals for the first five years of her life.

CHAPTER SIX

THE DECISION

CHAPTER SIX—The Decision

When my baby was about three months old, my mom helped me get an apartment. I was so happy to finally have my own space with no one around, standing over me, and no kind of living arrangements. By this time, I had begun to get very curious about being with women, and I ended up messing around with a married woman, with whom I thought I was in love. I was so far gone in the head that I wanted to tell everyone. However, I was flip-flopping because I had a male friend who would visit me from time to time. I was so caught up with this woman, that I had stopped taking my birth control shots, and because I was still having sex with a man I instantly became pregnant.

I was so afraid because my baby was only six months old and had several health issues. So, I decided I wouldn't tell anyone about my pregnancy and hid it from everyone. As the next nine months went on, I did all I could to conceal my pregnancy. No one ever knew or could tell that I was pregnant. After giving birth, I did not keep my baby son, I gave him up, and the rest of that year I became very depressed. I would have nightmares, I began to see things in my apartment, and I couldn't sleep at night. Once again, I started hanging around people who smoked and drank all the time, and I was drawn right back to it. I even started to take prescription sleeping pills that weren't mine. I lived with the regret of my actions. My baby was adopted by a couple, and the only thing I knew about him is his name. I was so depressed that I didn't even care about life anymore. I felt like I had committed a terrible sin and would never get into heaven. I also spoke death over my own life and spoke out loud, "that one day God was going to shut my womb up for the terrible thing I had done." I figured that God had turned his back on me for my sin and was going to send me to hell

Confessions of a Preacher's Daughter

for my actions. I continued my bisexual acts, smoking weed, popping pills, drinking and going to the club every weekend.

At this point, you as the reader may say to yourself, "wow! Why would she write all this stuff about herself for the world to know, she has this tell-all book." but I knew I had to tell this because of what a Prophetess told me one night at church. She told me I must tell my testimony word for word.

The tongue can bring death or life; those who love to talk will reap the consequences. (Proverbs 18:21 NLT)

CHAPTER SEVEN

MY EXPOSURE

CHAPTER SEVEN—My Exposure

SUMMER 2005

The summer of 2005 is the summer I started getting along with my mother for the first time in a long time. I was sitting in my bedroom one day, and it hit me that my mother never had the chance to feel and experience the love of a mother because her mother passed away when she was only two years old. I instantly felt terrible for blaming my mother for all my mistakes, so I started hanging around and talking to her more. I was even able to forgive my father for the beatings and the way he treated me while I was growing up. To this day I love my parents very much, and I am so glad I was able to push past the tumultuous childhood I had.

One day, I was at the store shopping, and I ran into an old flame of mine. He gave me his number, and we began to talk and spend time together. We were together off and on for a little over a year. I wanted to be serious with him, but I couldn't seem to stop seeing other men. I had the mindset of, "What one won't do, I will find one who will."

I still wasn't getting money from them, because it was their time and attention that I wanted. As my pastor taught about soul ties, I realized I was tied to this man, and he was tied to me. It was impossible to get this guy out of my mind and out of my heart. I began to talk about marriage to him. I became convinced that I was ready to settle down and have a family, but I wasn't, and neither was he. A few years later my eyes were opened to much about him. He would have been dating both my childhood best friend and me at the same time and then married her with a ring that he presented to me.

The Lord began to deal with me during the next few years; really, he had been speaking to me way before I started listening to him, but God had told me if I didn't get it

Confessions of a Preacher's Daughter

together that he was going to allow something to happen to me and I would die. You may be asking did I listen, well the answer was yes and no, in my heart I knew that He would allow my life to end before I wanted it to stop. Sometimes I would tell my boyfriend that I wasn't going to be around much longer if I didn't get it together.

So, I decided to go back to my church, and I became involved and started helping with the youth department. That's when exposure took place in my life. I was out there in the world, but I put my church face on around the church family. So, the Lord said, "Ok I will show you."

August 2007's Gunshots

It was my 27th birthday, and I began drinking early that day. My cousin, god-sister, and I went out to the club that night. My boyfriend even came out to see me. Once we got into the club, I took in more drinks. My boyfriend was not a dancer, so I got upset with him because he was playing pool with some old drunk man and wouldn't dance with me. I guess I got up under his skin, so he stuffed some money down my shirt, called me ungrateful, and left me standing there. Those of you, who know me, know that I hate being embarrassed in front of a lot of people, so I sat down and started crying. There I was, drunk as ever and crying on my birthday with everyone asking what was wrong.

My god-sister got up and pulled me to the dance floor to get my mind off what had happened. Her tactic didn't work because after the song went off and we started walking back to our seats, she didn't realize that I went out the door. As I walked out the door, I called my boyfriend on my cell phone. As soon as I got out the front door, a guy was stand-

CHAPTER SEVEN—My Exposure

ing there, and he started talking to me, then suddenly I saw a light flash, heard a pop.

The next thing I knew a guy that was a well-known nurse who had been in the club was leaning over me with a knife in his hand. I was on the ground with blood all over my arm, and I felt a very hot burning sensation in it. I realized the guy that was leaning over me was trying to cover up my wound because he had torn his shirt to tie it around my wound to stop the bleeding. I was so intoxicated that I didn't realize I had been shot until the shock to my body wore off, then I then began to panic.

The ambulance came and picked me up. By the time, I got to the ER, my mom, dad, stepmom, my now deceased older brother, and boyfriend where all at the hospital. I was embarrassed at myself for the mess in which I had accidentally entangled myself. The bullet hit me in my left shoulder and went back out the same shoulder, and to show you how God will send a word of confirmation thru anyone; a female doctor came in and sat down next to my bed, and she looked at me for a long time in silence before speaking. She said, "Tameka, do you know how many young folks come in here with gunshot wounds and they don't make it, do you know how blessed you are to be alive? You got all these people up here who love you, and God must really love you." She stared at me for a few more minutes and walked out of the room. This doctor's words pierced my heart, and I felt even more shame than I had when I first got to the ER.

The ER sent me home with some pain pills and antibiotics. The next morning, I woke up and felt like I had been hit by a train. A police officer came to question me about the incident. It turns out that I had walked right into a fight between two dudes outside the club. I walked right in the middle of flying bullets, and I was so drunk that I wasn't aware of my surroundings. By that Monday it was on the front page of the paper. I was so embarrassed to go back to church after that, but I knew then, that I had to be exposed to wake up.

As the days went on, I realized that I could have bled to death, or the bullet could have hit me in the head or the heart because I got hit on the left side. I don't know how long I was on the ground before someone found me, and the whole time I didn't even realize I was out. It showed me how fast your life could be snatched from you without the chance to say, "Lord save me, please forgive me, I accept you as my savior." See not all people have that chance, and I knew then that it was time to start making a change in my life. So I made a vow to start trying to live my life right, and it was a complicated process for me. I went right back to that same club, but this time when I went, I instantly felt convicted for being there. After the second time I went back after being shot, I didn't go back to that club again.

CHAPTER SEVEN—My Exposure

Have mercy on me O God, because of your unfailing love. Because of your compassion, blot out the stains of my sins. Wash me clean from my guilt. Purify me from me sin. For I recognize my rebellion; it haunts me day and night. Against you, and you alone, have I sinned; I have done what is evil in your sight. You will be proved right in what you say, and your judgment against me is just. For I was born a sinner- yes from the moment my mother conceived me. But you desire honesty from the womb, teaching me wisdom even there. Purify me from me sins and I will be clean, wash me and I will be whiter than snow. O, give me back my joy again; you have broken me-now let me rejoice. Don't keep looking at my sins. Remove the stain of my guilt. Create in me a clean heart, O God. Renew a loyal spirit within me. Do not banish me from your presence and don't take your Holy Spirit from me. Restore to me the joy of your salvation and make me willing to obey you. Then I will teach your ways to rebels, and they will return to you. Forgive me for shedding blood, O, God who saves; and then I will joyfully sing your forgiveness. Unseal my lips, O Lord, that my mouth may praise you. You do not desire a sacrifice, or I would offer one. You do not want a burnt offering. The sacrifice you desire is a broken spirit. You will not reject a broken and repentant heart O, God.
Psalms 51:1-17

CHAPTER EIGHT

LIES & SHAME

CHAPTER EIGHT — Lies & Shame

I finally stopped all the nonsense and club hopping. My so-called boyfriend was still lying to me about him seeing other women, so I started to push him away. It didn't seem to be working until I ran into an old friend from the 5th grade on the internet. We began talking and found out that we had a lot in common. We developed feelings for each other, and by the end of the year, we decided to start dating. It seemed very complicated because he lived in North Carolina and I lived in Arkansas. So over the next few months, we flew back and forth to see each other. I had even decided to leave Arkansas to move out there with him. I moved out of my house and moved in with my mother. Instantly, the Lord said, "No." But as usual, I ignored him.

One Sunday, I decided I was tired of running from God, and I went and rededicated my life to Him. I told my boyfriend about it, but he informed me that he wasn't ready to change yet, and we may need to stop seeing each other as much because he didn't want to be the reason I fell back into the world. Well, I got upset and called the whole relationship off. He was pretty angry with me and told me he never said that he didn't want me.

Throughout my life, I had hurt men and hurt myself, because I always felt the one I was dating wasn't good enough for me, or I just wasn't happy with anyone. I was perplexed at this time because I still had my ex-boyfriend bothering me, trying to play my ex-best friend and me against one another. He bad-mouthed me to her and lied so much to both of us that she didn't even want to be my friend anymore. She refused to believe he had been dating both of us.

One day, I was in Applebee's with a church sister and a lady who knew him was there. She told me some news that

Confessions of a Preacher's Daughter

sent me off my rocker. According to her, the same engagement ring he had shown me one week before, my best friend from grade school was now wearing it. I called him and asked him about it, and of course, he denied it and never told me the truth. Well, this was the straw that broke the camel's back for me. I expressed to him that out of all the things I'd done and that he had done, I would never have done something like that to him. I couldn't believe what he had done, so I sought out to get back at him.

Now, here I was making the same mistake I had repeatedly made. I was dating, but I was still having sex, and I would jump from man to man and not give myself time to heal before moving on to the next man. It left me very confused about what I ever wanted from a man or what kind of husband I desired.

I never really knew what it was like to live a saved Christian life as a single woman. I knew at the time that's what God wanted from me, but I ignored him and still went and did what I wanted to do. And yes, I got whipped for being disobedient. There's no whipping like one from God! The Lord had spoken to me and told me to stop having sex, and to cut off connections with the men I had been dating. But as stubborn as I was, I didn't listen and went and jumped right on into another relationship with a new guy.

I began to use this guy to try to heal the hurt I had in my heart. I didn't know where I had left my heart, but I was desperately trying to find it. I didn't know if it was in North Carolina, or if my ex-boyfriend had it. So, I began to use God as an excuse to get the guy to marry me. I knew I wasn't ready. The Lord had even spoken to me to wait before I got married because I needed to sow a season of abstinence to him, but I still kept on having sex up until the day I got the

CHAPTER EIGHT—Lies & Shame

guy to say yes he would marry me. We got married. I had a miscarriage a month after we got married, but I didn't know I was pregnant or when I had gotten pregnant.

The miscarriage was due to a fall I had taken at a paintball ranch. After the fall, I started having some pains in my back. The next week I began to bleed heavy for about ten days. A few months after that, my pastor prophesied to me that God was getting ready to open my womb up, physically. I was very excited, and I thanked God for I knew he had closed my womb up for the evil thing I had done. Now I would just wait on Him to manifest it.

~God often chose infertility as a precursor to the birth of a promised child or unique child, marking the birth as God's work. God's delays are not necessarily denials, but they remind longing parents to use trials for growth and to see children as a gift that cannot be taken for granted. ~

CHAPTER NINE

PERSECUTION & CONFUSION

CHAPTER NINE—Persecution & Confusion

The enemy began to taunt me by using other people around me to the point that I started being persecuted for going to church by a supervisor at work. She would talk about me going to church and call me church girl so much until it would have me so mad that I could barely work without an attitude. She would talk about me on Sundays if I bought my dress clothes to work with me for evening programs I was going to after my shift was over. There were times when she would even call my clothes sanctified and make jokes about dancing in church. Most of the time, I couldn't even sit down at lunch for her harassing me. Then at the end of the day, she would say she was only joking around with me. My other bosses over her did nothing about it. They had already told me that if my religion was going to hinder my job, then I didn't need to be there. She eventually stopped talking to me because she said I so-called threw her under the bus by complaining to our boss.

God blesses you when people mock you, persecute you, lie about you, and say all sorts of evil things against you because you are one of his followers. Be happy about it! Be very glad! For a great reward awaits you in heaven. And remember the ancient prophets were persecuted in the same way. (Matthew 5:11-12 NLT)

My test and trials became extremely heavy, and the enemy began to work on me so bad in my mind, that I couldn't tell anyone what was going on. I felt like I was about to lose my mind. I began to feel as if I was falling into an abyss and started regretting the fact that I got married. I was starting to wish I had listened to God and waited. So, since I didn't follow what I knew ahead of time, I began to pray and ask God to allow me to love my husband as I should.

Confessions of a Preacher's Daughter

My older brother died from an illness on the morning of Fathers Day in 2009. It came as a big shock to me as I got the call and had just got off an early morning flight from a conference I had attended. It hurt my heart so badly I could not even pay attention to the service that morning. I felt sorry for my dad because no parent wants to have to bury their child; they would rather the child bury them.

It wasn't until October 2009, at a women's conference in Washington D.C., that I found out some things about myself. There was a minister there who spoke to me and began to tell me about all these generational curses in my family, and more specifically, how the women in my family were cursed. She began to call different evil spirits out of me, and during this time I started to purge all these unclean things. It was a feeling I would never forget. I felt different and stronger. I didn't feel as bound anymore, and it was a relief to find out after so many years what had me bound.

The minister told me that demons had been assigned to me since birth to torment me in my mind. She called the spirit of depression out of me, and she told me if I wanted deliverance I had to make a release. I began to cry out to God, and as I did, I started to feel light. As she began to call these spirits out, I could feel myself choking, and I knew this was the beginning of my purge. Before I left, the Prophetess told my First Lady that she saw pregnancy all over me. I was like wow, maybe the promise is coming soon.

Purify me from my sins, and I will be clean; wash me, and I will be whiter than snow. (Psalms 50:7 NLT)

When I left that conference, I felt like a different person. My eyes and ears opened more, spiritually. When I got

CHAPTER NINE—Persecution & Confusion

back, I was tested, again. During this season, I lost friends, and church family who I thought were for me, but my ears were opened up to the conversations. The enemy tried to use this against me by speaking to me telling me to leave the ministry because no one cares about me there. He began to say to me there was no purpose in life for me and that God had no need for me. Not too long after that, I was talking with my mom, and she shared some things with me about my family. My mother informed me a prophetess told her that she had been cursed.

Now to show you how God works, not too long after she told me this the woman revealed herself to my mom. I was very shocked. This woman, who was heavily into witchcraft, was a friend of my great grandmother. She said to my mom, "Yeah ask your grandmother, I can control anyone." My mom even told me about how my grandmother told her on several occasions that she wished snakes would crawl into me and my cousin's mouth as babies, and suck the milk out of us. In disbelief, I questioned, "She spoke death over me as a baby?"

A lot of people don't believe in witchcraft or being possessed by evil spirits. My mom shared with me how I acted like a child, and she and my father believed that I was possessed. When you leave the door open, those spirits will dwell there and then invite in more in. As a child, I remember seeing things and things were on me that I couldn't see. I also remember images talking to me, but as a small child, I didn't know any better. That's why we must make sure our houses are in order because we never know what we are putting our kids in danger. When you learn how spirits work, you will understand them and be able to crucify them at the root.

Confessions of a Preacher's Daughter

Familiar spirits are demonic agents whose primary assignment is to become well acquainted with a person or groups of persons. They are responsible for satanic surveillance. They gather information on you and use your weaknesses against you. They know you so well that they can imitate you and produce deception. Deception comes from confederations to attack the people of God. They know your every dislike and like. Their job is to stop the plan of God.

They have these assignments
1. *Geographical - regions (Mark 5:1-10)*
2. *Individual - can start a cultural assignment, (1st Samuel 28:3-9, 1st Chronicles 10:13)*
3. *Cultural - (generational curses) - families, (Numbers 33:50-55)*

I soon began to feel like I didn't want to be married anymore. I was tired of my husband being complacent and not providing as he should, so I began to shut myself out and away from him because I was tired of telling him what I thought he should be doing. The feelings that I had been trying to conceal were starting to show. The situation with my husband was starting to drive me up the wall, and I began to fuss and complained about everything that I thought he should have been doing a long time before then. Yes, he should have been doing it, but as a wife, we can't beat our husbands down because it will make them feel less of a man. A certain elder told me that I should pray about it and give it to God if my husband isn't doing what he supposed to do; but if I badger the man, God will deal with me also.
One Sunday some of the members at my church were talking about a dream my pastor had about two women at the

CHAPTER NINE—Persecution & Confusion

church being pregnant. I wondered if it was because my period was late, but I didn't want to get too excited, so I tried to put the thought out of my head. My spiritual sister texted me one day and told me to buy a pregnancy test, so I went and got one and took it; sure enough, it was positive. I felt like ok God here's the promise you gave me, and it has come to pass and as soon as I told everyone I lost the baby.

The next four days I had a miscarriage. The loss of another child before birth broke my spirit because I didn't understand why this had happened again, twice in 9 months. I questioned God and asked Him, "Is this my punishment for not keeping my son?" I went into another unseen depression and started pushing my husband away. The more I looked at my husband and his laziness and the things I felt he should be doing as a man, the more I despised him. I became so rooted in getting out of my marriage that by the end of November, I had gotten him to leave. He stayed gone four days, but I let him come back home. Not because I wanted him to, but because my Pastor and First Lady had convinced me to do so. I did everything I could to stay away from him and make him leave. I had made my mind up that I was ready to be single again because I still felt like I was living like I was single. My husband wasn't acting as the man, or even the husband I thought he should be, so I figured that I might as well make it official.

My mindset had changed entirely, and I didn't care what my church family thought. I had even prepared myself to leave the church if they didn't want to accept my decision. I felt like it's my life and not theirs, I make my own choices. So at bible study, one night, the Prophetess at the church began speaking to me, and before I knew it, we were all in spiritual warfare. The Prophetess told me that I was cursed since I was a child. She also told me there had been so much witchcraft in my family, that different spirits had attached themselves to me. They had been there for so long that they had rooted themselves in me, and that's why I couldn't get my deliverance. She spoke in my ear about my testimony and that I had to tell it word for word. The minister at church let me know that the enemy wanted to use what I was going through to pull me back into the world, but only to take me out.

But be careful don't let your heart be deceived so that you turn away from the Lord and serve and worship other gods. If you do, the Lord's anger will burn against you. He will shut up the sky, and hold back the rain, and the ground will fail to produce its harvest. Then you will quickly die in that good land the Lord is giving you.
　　　　Deuteronomy 11:16-17 NLT

　　　I was instructed to take a three day fast. During these three days, I did a lot of thinking and talking to God. I asked him to forgive me of all my sins and to heal me of the shame and hurt I had carried for many years. So, I cut off the connection I had with the other men I had been talking to, and I started doing some soul searching.
　　　I asked God to remove all the things that had me bound and cursed since I was a child. My memory went back to my mom telling me that she and my dad felt like I was possessed as a child and that she sometimes was afraid of me. I also thought about how my life had been up until the present time, and I said, "Oh my God, that's why I have always been, set back."

CHAPTER NINE—Persecution & Confusion

The minister reminded me of everything I had been through and how the devil had used me and been at my footsteps since I entered the world. It was because he was trying to stop the anointing that was over my life and did everything he could to keep me from walking in it. During my three day fast, I began to pray and ask God to give me a new heart and renew my spirit. For so many years I never would face the fact that I didn't love myself. How can one love God, or anyone else, if they don't love self? I had to learn to love myself, and in the process, I asked God to help me to unhardened my heart so I could learn to how to love Him, and then myself.

CHAPTER TEN

THE SCENT OF A MAN

CHAPTER TEN—The Scent of a Man

I am sure you are thinking to yourself, What does she mean by the scent of a man? Father's Day is one of the most overlooked holidays, for a number reasons. The only one I will focus on is the lack of a father or the right father figure in a young girl's life. I can't help but wonder about those young girls who have no father in their life. How does life go when paternal protection, support, and fatherly love is missing from her life? Is she significantly impacted? "I believe she is." However, the question is, "What defines father?" Is it just a man who gave seed to produce fruit, one who only provides financial obligations, shelter & food, or is it one who provides all of the above, plus love, security, protection, and emotional support.

I go back to my own life a lot in this book, as my past life has been a huge learning cycle for me. Growing up in a two-parent home, I have always had a father figure in my life. I carry the name of a man I call my father, but I am not the fruit of his loin. So that leaves the man who is the reason I am here, whom I met when I was well over 30 years of age. The man that raised me and provide for me is the man I call my father. Yet I have a relationship with both of them, there is still something missing from my childhood. Something that is missing from a lot of girls and older women lives.

There is a saying, a woman can't teach her son how to be a man; only his father can accomplish that task. Well, a young girl needs a father in her life to teach her what love from a man is, to keep her from making a lot of mistakes when she begins to date and enter into relationships. The mistake a lot of men make with children is they have the mindset that as long as they are providing basic life survival needs, these acts qualify them as a father. This mindset is all

Confessions of a Preacher's Daughter

wrong. Children also need plenty of love and support from both parents. This mindset still leaves a child fatherless. Children go to school and can even be disruptive all through school all due to the lack of a father or father figure in their life because there is no guidance, no love, no father-son or father-daughter time both in and outside of the home.

What is Fatherlessness?

It is the lack of an emotional bond between a daughter and her father. A fatherless daughter can experience many silent emotional breakdowns, rendering them trauma survivors from a young age. The impact of this trauma affects her at every major developmental milestone of her life. Young girls can miss out on learning positive masculine behaviors, certain social skills and a comfort with male-female relationships because their fathers were not there to teach them. Which is what gave me the title, The Scent of Man.

Many women go through life and go from man to man, never being fully satisfied in a relationship because they don't know what to look for in a potential mate and for most when they do encounter a man who truly loves them, they don't know how to receive love, due to the fact they don't even recognize love from a man. Some women even unknowingly date and are attracted to men who are aggressive because they are still searching for that fatherly figure in a man. Most women who grew up without a father around find it hard to distinguish between LOVE and LUST from a man who is interested in her. Often, she is the type of woman who will hurt a man who is truly in love with her. She does not have the proper identity of a real man.

She does not have the scent of her father upon her.

CHAPTER TEN—The Scent of a Man

Little girls need a special kind of love growing up that only a father can give. Little girls need to be told how pretty they are, growing up, to help build up their self-esteem and self-image while they are young. They need a father in their life to take them out on dates and show them what to expect out of a good man. One to who will teach them how to know when they are dealing with an abusive or lazy man. Many people do not believe a person's upbringing has about 75% effect on their adulthood and the choices they make along the way.

A fatherless young woman can step into an unknown world and make many mistakes in relationships simply because she is missing something vital from her life. She may aimlessly look for a father in a man she's dating and always end the relationship in disaster. Ladies, your husband cannot be your father.

Many homes do have a father or father figure but he is not active in the children's lives, and this is why I say, "All children need more than just a provider in a father." You have to spend time and get to know the young adult your child is growing into, in order to help them become the women and men of our future.

I am stressing to any man reading this chapter, take the time out to be there for your daughters all through their lives. Be there for the dress up princess and prince games, be there for that first boyfriend breakup, be there to chase off that no good boyfriend, be there to open up her car door and a young age, and teach her what a good man looks for in a woman they are looking to be their wife. Teach them about how there are bad people out there that may want to hurt them sexually. Because your daughters need your scent all

Confessions of a Preacher's Daughter

on them, so later on in their life they will not settle for anything less than what they deserve from a man. So in closing guys, always leave your scent on your daughters.

Sometimes you have to go back to the past to embrace the future. All over the world, there is a 12-year-old girl in a 40-year-old body, just wishing for a hug from her daddy that she never received. She's 40 years old still longing to have memories of piggyback rides, daddy running off boyfriends, getting forehead kisses, and being told she is loved and pretty.

Wishing her daddy would have broken through the barrier of hurt inflicted upon her so many years ago, she wishes he would have seen the precious little girl that she was, but alas he was too blind to see his own faults. And now that little girl resides in a body and a mind that longs for a love that only a father can give.

So many broken women walking around and that small little girl is still hidden on the inside screaming out for help and love. Fathers love your daughters while they are young so they can grow into the women that will be able to receive love from a man and not lead a life of mistakes with men.

CHAPTER ELEVEN

ENOUGH IS ENOUGH

CHAPTER ELEVEN—Enough is Enough

Why do we love?

Is it our way of finding our place in this world, or finding someone who completes us?

Is it our search for a deeper connection, or we just afraid of being alone?

Does life still have meaning without love or trust?

What do you do when love is lost? Do you give up, or do you try to find love where it is lost before it's too late?

Why do we love?

Enough is Enough is a title that came to me one night while thinking back on my past relationships and mere friendships I have had. Many times, I found myself asking the question, "Why did I waste my time trying to be someone's friend," or "Why did I waste my time on this person?" Have you gotten to the point in your relationship that you are asking yourself these questions?

1. What in the world?
2. Why are you not the same person I met X number of months ago?
3. What have I got myself into?
4. Where is the love that you promised me? You picked a fine time to tell me that you didn't love me.

Pay attention to the signs! After the great sex and high life, reality sets in and if the other person has stopped doing whatever he or she did to get you; then they may not truly be in love with you. If you are asking these questions, this section may be for you and could be a great help to you.

Confessions of a Preacher's Daughter

While many people do not like to hear the truth, nor do they want to listen to spiritual advice. The advice throughout the book comes from my personal experiences and observing others in their relationships. The scripture references come directly from the Holy Bible. I hope by the time you read this in full you will be able to recognize some of the warning signs in time to get away from someone who may not be good for you. Furthermore, I hope my advice will help you avoid the potential headaches from the person with whom you are thinking about continuing in a relationship.

Peaches and Cream

Well, you finally meet someone who seems to be kind, sweet, and he or she fits your description of a decent person to date and see where it will lead. You see each other rather often and talk & text on the phone from sunup to sundown. You are feeling this person, and the two of you seem to be falling in love, fast. You have both introduced on another to your parents, family, and friends. Everyone admires your relationship, and you both boast about how you never fight and how you were made for each other.

We sometimes call this cupcake or the caking stage. The caking phase is the earliest phase of the honeymoon phase of a relationship.

When a couple is engaged in public displays of affection and/or being anti-social by only paying attention to one another during a social outing with a group of friends, or when a guy or a girl chooses to spend time with a love interest over their friends, they are usually in the caking phase.

CHAPTER ELEVEN—Enough is Enough

There is a lot of fun, playfulness, physical contact, sexual energy, and many of the bad habits and shortcomings are overlooked. Why? It is usually because one or both parties will have in mind that the person will change later on and that they are just in their beginning stage.

When we think we are in love, we feel different, and respond differently to our partner. In turn, this seems to cause our hearts to blind our ability to reason. This stage can bring you a false outlook on a possible happy future because you are only looking at the right now, you are solely focused on the good sex, the good looks, and nice-looking body. (Lust of the Eyes & Flesh) This stage in dating, for the most part, will usually last up to 3 to 12 months in just dating and will last up to 3 to 5 years in marriage.

Once reality sets in, things such as bills, unknown bad and low credit scores, overdue bills, repossessed vehicles, and how clean or nasty a person lives, etc. come to the forefront. If you do not take the time out to get to know a person and ask those questions that need to be asked, you will soon find yourself single or stuck paying thousands of dollars and even more in time, for a divorce. Get to know who you are dating before you jump head first and heart wide open.

Don't get caught up expecting him to buy you a ring or expecting her to be the girl you take home to meet mom if he/she doesn't know how to love you! No matter how much pressure social media or every kiss begins with K posts put on you, allow them time to grow with GOD! And if he/she doesn't have a relationship with GOD, you'll end up saying all men/women are the same. Why? Because YOU FORCED SOMETHING THAT WASN'T THERE.

Confessions of a Preacher's Daughter

Who Are You

So now that reality has set in, and the cupcaking stage is over, you find yourself staring into the face of a monster. That person is no longer the person you met six months ago. And now you're wondering who the hell YOU are anymore... You've lost yourself in the midst of trying to find or be with someone else.

I hope to help you determine that some things are beyond your control of being able to change. At the end of the day, it's your choice to stay or leave a person who has apparently evolved into a different person. You have to self-evaluate first before you go pointing the blame on your so-called boo thang.

You really don't want to become a Husband/Wife if...

1. You're not ready to be in the position to forgive or need forgiveness.

2. You're not ready to walk him/her through feelings that neither of you understand.

3. You, like a bird, are so addicted to the warm seasons of life that you'd fly south for the winter and you can NEVER be pleased.

4. You're not willing to be humble enough to apologize when you're wrong.

5. You'd rather him/her go through whatever their going through alone and then just show up when it's over.

6. You have no intention of adjusting yourself. Knowing that you can only change YOU.

CHAPTER ELEVEN—Enough is Enough

7. You only want financial security.

8. You've convinced yourself that he/she will remain exactly as they are today.

9. You only want to spend time on the playground and not the classroom.

10. You only want him/her RIGHT NOW.

11. You can't see the value you bring or the value that's brought to you by the relationship.

12. You want the full package TODAY.

Did you know there are just as many scriptures that instruct a husband on how to behave in a marriage as there are instructions for the wife? The world and the church will focus most if not all the weight on the wife to fix a broken or failing marriage.

We tell the wife to create a peaceful atmosphere, but the husband may be the one to bring the negative energy, making it hostile a hostile environment. People will say, "Oh it's just a man being a man. Be submissive and wait for him to change." All the while, he picks and chooses what he wants to be the head of and when he wants to be the head. The bible says both husband and wife are to submit to each other.

Confessions of a Preacher's Daughter

The Bible teaches neither spouse's body belongs to self, it belongs to the spouse. So, why is it when the husband refuses sex and intimacy with his wife, and she commits adultery, it's all her fault she cheated on her husband? The Bible also teaches against withholding sex from a spouse. However, we make up excuses for the husband, "Oh he can't perform under stress... or he can't have sex after an argument." The Bible also teaches to not let the sun go down on your anger. We as a people need to stop the pressuring of the wife to do all the Bible says, but make excuses for why the husband is not doing what the Bible tells him to do.

I honestly believe some women turn to bad habits like drinking, drugs, promiscuity, acting out, and abusive behaviors towards self, the children, and husband. The world and the church have told her she had to stay and deal with a husband who is clearly showing her he does not want her anymore. There is no such thing in my book as, I don't want you right now, but maybe later. No ma'am. No sir. If he/she is showing you through their actions, then you are the fool for staying. You don't stay just because a book said stay or your pastor told you that you have to stay. That book and pastor don't live with you and know everything that goes on behind your closed doors.

At the end of the day, the decision you make is between you and God. Never let the world or the church brainwash you into driving yourself insane trying to fix a marriage in which the other party refuses to help fix what they took part in breaking. Stop using specific Bible scriptures to hang over the wife's head, and not do the same to the husband. In conclusion, the only way a marriage cannot be rebuilt is if the wife or husband are refusing to cooperate or

CHAPTER ELEVEN—Enough is Enough

compromise with one another. It takes two to destroy a marriage. So, it's going to take two to repair it.

Ephesians 5:25: "For husbands, this means love your wives, just as Christ loved the church. He gave up his life for her." Genesis 2:24: "Therefore a man shall leave his father and his mother and hold fast to his wife, and they shall become one flesh." ... He who loves his wife loves himself.

Proverbs 14:1 The wise woman builds her house, But the foolish pulls it down with her hands.

1st Corinthians 7:2-5 (NKJV) 2) nevertheless, because of sexual immorality, let each man have his own wife, and let each woman have her own husband. 3)Let the husband render to his wife the affection due her, and likewise also the wife to her husband. 4) The wife does not have authority over her own body, but the husband does. And likewise the husband does not have authority over his own body, but the wife does. 5) Do not deprive one another except with consent for a time that you may give yourselves to fasting and prayer; and come together again so that Satan does not tempt you because of your lack of self-control.

Soul Ties

The wrong relationship can take away from your destiny! To be a holy and righteous young man and woman, you may still reach your goals if you are in the wrong relationship, but only with many unnecessary heartaches, detours, and delays. A soul tie with the wrong person hinders your purpose and destiny, and it acts as an entry for others negative spirits. These spirits steal innocence, purity, and focus.

Confessions of a Preacher's Daughter

There are six ways soul ties can be made:

1. **Marriage:** When deciding to get married, you must be sure your chosen spouse is who God desires for you. Sometimes he will not stop you, and he will let you marry someone just to show you how to wait on when he says to marry. Once you marry, you will have sex and sometimes children. At this point, you have not only joined yourself sexually with someone, but you have joined your blood for generations to come through the children you produce with them.

2. **Friendship:** There comes a time in everyone's life when a person chooses to live for God. He will tell you to break free of certain friends. Sometimes, he will allow something to happen to cause a separation, or he will instruct you to cut some people lose. Because they are not a part of your destiny, they will only delay or become a distraction to what he is trying to do in certain areas of your life, especially spiritually.

3. **Family:** soul ties can be made as a child grows, due to the parents raising children a certain way and that child grows in to an adult and finds out that the way they was taught, was not the right upbringing, but their parents teaching is so rooted in them that they may find it very hard to break certain habits. For instance, a woman has four sons, and her husband abused her all the time; at least one of those sons will grow up and abuse their wife, or they let their wife abuse them. Why? Because that's all they grew up with and that's all they know, and once they realize it's wrong, it becomes a bad habit that is hard to break.

4. **Sexual partners:** To be blunt about it, every person you have ever had sexual intercourse with you connected with them as one. Sex is sex. No matter if the acts occur or you

CHAPTER ELEVEN—Enough is Enough

participate in other areas of bedroom activity. Sexual intercourse is for marriage. When a man and a woman join their self in the act of sex, they become one. Women have sexual soul ties with other men because God made the woman the receiver, the carrier, and nurturer of the seed that gets planted through the act of sex. Therefore, many women become obsessed with men. Often, once they have been kicked to the curb after having sex with a man, it becomes tough for that woman to let go of the man because she has joined her body and her spirit with a man who is not her husband. To my young ladies, keep your virtue until marriage, keep yourself pure because God will greatly reward you for being faithful to him.

5. **Demonic forces:** Many people say they do not believe in witchcraft. Witchcraft is just a name given to define the act of people who worship Satan, those who call on him for prophecies, and for power to harm and control others. In the book of Deuteronomy, God gave laws to stay away from people who practice these type of acts. When you have a family that has practiced these evil acts, they invite Satan and his demons to enter their bodies to gain strength or power. Thus, when they decided they don't want to practice it anymore, Satan and his demons make it extra hard to seek deliverance from God, because a person has such evilness rooted in their spirits.

6. Organizational groups:
    - Organized Traditional Religious Groups
    - Secret organizations
    - Cults
    - Sororities, Fraternities

Confessions of a Preacher's Daughter

I know I will make someone mad with this, but hey, I'm going to say it anyway. You should be very careful when joining groups, because you may not know the full origin behind it, what it's all about, or what kind of practices the group originally did when founded. Most organized groups use God as a crutch, to try and justify what they are doing within the group, by including prayer or quoting scriptures. Remember, Satan was once an angel of the Lord. He too can quote scriptures, pray, sing, worship, and praise God.

Many groups, especially religious denominational groups, each have their own set rules. They each boast of what they feel is right and wrong to do in a church house. Many have rules on how to praise and worship, and some are against dance and music. You have some that seem to be more worried about money than saving lives. Therefore, many churches are spiritually dead, and the Holy Spirit doesn't dwell anywhere in their temples. Some churches have their members so spiritually and mentally messed up in the head that while the members may not agree with what the organization is doing, they are so caught up in the system that they end up staying.

The members don't even believe in the principles of the organization and end up on the road to hell. So, while they know better spiritually, they decide on staying bound up, because they don't know how to break ties with organized religion.

Guard your eyes, your ear, and your mind, always! Satan gets to us the most often because we are listening to, we are looking at, or we have become so high minded that we can no longer hear or recognize the voice of God. Everything outside of your purpose is a stumbling block for you to lose focus of the road God has set before you to walk.

CHAPTER ELEVEN—Enough is Enough

If you are having problems with your flesh, it's time to put your mind and body into a spiritual rehab, by doing some fasting, praying, and repenting to get your deliverance from SELF. If your eyes are a hindrance, then stop yourself from looking at what you know is wrong, AND stop your ears from listening to what you know is wrong. If what someone is saying to you has you all jacked up in the head, stop listening to them. Never be too proud to ask God for help, and never be too proud to ask for help from someone who can help you get to your deliverance.

Two gates to your soul and body for the enemy to come through
1. **Lust of the flesh**
2. **Lust of the eyes**

CHAPTER TWELVE

THE TONGUE

CHAPTER TWELVE—The Tongue

If God judged everyone based on sins and mistakes, we all would be dead! So, why do we judge people when they make mistakes? There is always room for change, and if there is a God, then anyone can change. We need to stop judging others, speaking death over them, and nailing them to the cross. We need to be encouraging them instead of tearing them down with our tongues. Because we have no heaven or hell to which can condemn anyone if we see someone is having a problem or they have committed wrongdoing, we should not be so quick to criticize and condemn them. When we put our mouth on them to their face or behind their back, it only tears them down more than what they are doing to their self.

Proverbs 18:21 says, "Death and life are in the power of the tongue: and they that love it shall eat the fruit thereof." The words we speak, are they words of LIFE or words of DEATH? Do they give us hope or discouragement?

Has anyone ever said something negative to you, and you just wilted and felt like you had died inside? Perhaps they said some beautiful words to you, and then you just blossomed like a flower. According to scripture, this is the way of the tongue. Let us, therefore, tend to life with our tongue, which may seem to be an impossible task; but be assured with God all things are possible (Mark 9:23). We will and shall be able to tame the tongue and only speak living words of life and reality.

In Proverbs 26:20 we also find these words: "Where no wood is, there the fire goes out: so where there is no talebearer, the strife ceases." When our wood, hay, and stubble are consumed, the carnal fire has gone out, but the eternal flame of God will burn forever.

Confessions of a Preacher's Daughter

"And the tongue is a fire, a world of iniquity: so is the tongue among our members, that it defiles the whole body, and sets on fire the course of nature; and is set on fire of hell, for every kind of beast, and of birds, and of serpents, and of things in the sea, is tamed, and hath been tamed of mankind: But the tongue can no man tame; it is an unruly evil, full of deadly poison."

Therewith bless God, even the Father; and therewith curse we men, which are made after the similitude of God. Out of the same mouth proceeded blessing and cursing. My brethren, these things ought not so to be. Doth a fountain send forth at the same place sweet water and bitter?" (Jms.3:6-11).

It doesn't matter what someone has done to you or what someone is doing; we should not kill them with our mouths. If you can't come to them and say, "Brother or sister, let me pray with you and for you for your deliverance," then do not speak death over them by telling them they will never change. You are not God. With God all things are possible.

When we begin to speak death over others, it is a form of witchcraft, and the more we speak negatively of others, the more we start to speak these negative things into existence. I, myself, try to be careful with my words when I am angry or upset with someone. During angered times our tongues work the most negativity, and it is also the time when we tend to say the first and most hurtful things that come to our minds. I learned one of the meanings of this in a psychology class. When we do this, it's called "transfer of emotions off one to another." Meaning, whatever a person has done to us we want to try to make them feel the hurt that they have caused us. So we do this with that little pink thing in our mouths.

CHAPTER TWELVE—The Tongue

Even when we know what we are saying will hurt the person, we still go forth with letting the hurt flow out of our mouths. Sometimes a person can be such a good friend, sister, brother, cousin, boyfriend, or girlfriend that they can kill you with one sentence from their lips there is another saying that "actions speak louder than words." Well, that's a two-sided statement because no matter how good of a person someone may show you they are, when they get angry with you, their mouth begins to speak things that can instantly bring tears to your eyes. You feel as if that person has slapped you in the face, or they have taken a dagger and pierced through to your soul.

Let us pray for our tongues to be tamed, so we will not tear someone down even more. Many people are already bound, being an enemy to their self, or have fallen into spiritual death. At the end of the day, when we stop and think of the wrongs we do on a daily basis if you or the person you're talking down on died right now in the middle of your sins, without the chance to repent, you both would be condemned to a burning hell.

As when the men of the village brought the woman to Jesus to stone her, and as he began to write in the sand, he only spoke these words, "He that is without sin cast the first stone." All of the men disappeared before he finished writing. I believe he was writing down sins that each of them committed.

When we are angry, we should not sin, in our words, actions, or deeds. I am not saying we should not ever be upset or express the hurt that someone else has caused us. Nor am I saying we should not hold one another accountable. However, it's important how you say whatever you say to the person.

Confessions of a Preacher's Daughter

And if we are to go to others with a person's issues, it should not be to gossip, but to gather together and pray for the individual. Let us pray for the heart of God to enter into us so we will view others through the eyes of God and not our own eyes.

CHAPTER THIRTEEN

WHY ARE YOU JUDGING?

CHAPTER THIRTEEN—Why Are You Judging?

Time after time I hear very common statements about people, which consist of he or she used to do this and that, or don't fool with that person, because they used to be a certain way. So many people are judged by their past ways, failures, and accomplishments. I recently had a statement made to me that made me stop and think about what people think about me.

I know the way I used to be; how I used to be out in the world, clubbing, smoking and whoring with whomever, I chose. Yes! A change did take place in my life, but it didn't happen overnight. And, upon changing my life I can say that I haven't stumbled along the way, but it's the God in me that keeps me from going back into the world.

I am a freelance writer and blogger. Most people who have a blogger's writing style have to ability to write about anything. Much of what they may write about is from personal experiences. While some people may not like what they write about, 9 times out of 10, it's about subject that needs to be talked about, publicly.

Now, own to my point. I recently made a decision that changed my spiritual walk, not with God but with Man. And upon my doing this, I was quickly the center of some people's conversation.

I really didn't care about it because I know how people can be when they are left in the dark about something that's none of their business. Well-being that I am a writer; I find it very easy to express myself through the written word. I can transfer my thoughts on to a piece of paper or in a blog with ease.

Confessions of a Preacher's Daughter

I put up a question on Facebook some time ago for a few thoughts from other people before I submitted my piece to a company. I guess I offended a few people they quickly took what they thought was bait or I was being funny and made a status on their page directed at me. It was hilarious to me at first, but then I became angry because I didn't understand how to exercise my gift of writing, ask for their input on certain subjects, and do so without being ridiculed.

I made a vow to God that I would only write about things to help people in their everyday lives and please him. I quickly deleted some people off my page and waited for my phone to start ringing. Sure enough, it rang, and I got text messages. I responded and told one person to leave me alone and to stop being messy because they were supposed to be "saved." Instead of asking me what I meant by what I wrote, I became the joke of their conversation on Facebook.

Instead of ignoring this person's text messages, I responded to each one. One text, in particular, stuck with me. The note read, "You need help with all your lustful spirits." Immediately, I was taken aback and felt even more vexed than before. I wondered how the fellow church could say such a thing about me because of a decision I made. And be it told, they didn't have the slightest clue as to why I made this decision. But, since they knew of my past, they decided I had fallen and went back into my old ways. Instead of this person encouraging me, the stones they were once throwing at my back, they were now throwing them right in my face. I wasn't the least bit shocked at this behavior because I expected it, and if I were a weak person I would have went into a shell.

CHAPTER THIRTEEN—Why Are You Judging?

Now some may wonder why I am sharing this... Well, it's not to expose anyone. I am sharing this to say we must not judge people based on their past. If we look at our life path, we would see that we have skeletons in our closets. And to the church folks, you all have no excuses to judge your sisters and brothers just because they had a past of acting out or whatever. Secondly, if you even think someone has fallen, it's not your business to get together with the next person laughing and talking about them. This kind of behavior only shows you need some major self-growth yourself.

The church is the main place sinners come running to as a safe place and as a door to God. However, the church can't help them if time the sinner run in their door, they running back out the door because someone has wronged them and stabbed them in the back by judging them, spreading their business, or laughing in their face.

I was very hurt and upset at this incident. But after some prayer, I thought about how I could worship with people who only smile in my face. Then, they laugh not only behind your back, but they mock you in your face.

We must not continue this kind of behavior in the church, because it will only run off the same people you're trying to save. Where is the sinner supposed to go if they can't even trust the church folks? As an old saying goes "you can't judge a book by its cover." As Christians, we need to stop saying someone has gone back to their old ways, creating assumptions as to why someone is having a midlife crisis, why they have lost everything, or why they walk away from people.

How can anyone be your support system, and when troubles arise in your life, they mock you, lie on you, laugh in your face, or call you to harass you? When is the madness going to stop? I pray for people to get saved for real and learn what "shut up" means.

Again, don't put your mouth on other's situation when you have no idea what's going on. I say this boldly to those type of people, "Get saved for real with yawl messy saved selves! Stop spreading lies about people!" I pray that when you began to put your mouth on others that God shuts your mouth up!

CHAPTER FOURTEEN

TEMPTATIONS

CHAPTER FOURTEEN—Temptations

Blessed is the man that endured temptation: for when he is tried, he shall receive the crown of life, which the Lord hath promised to them that love him.13) Let no man say when he is tempted, I am tempted of God: for God cannot be tempted with evil, neither tempted he any man: 14) But every man is tempted, when he is drawn away of his lust, and enticed.15) Then when lust hath conceived, it bringeth forth sin: and sin, when it is finished, bringeth forth death.
James 1: 12-15 KJV

Sometimes I sit back, think over my life, and look at how I easily fell into temptations. It was just as my momma sitting a plate of cookies on the table and telling me not to eat one, and as soon as she turned her back, I-ate-one. Seriously!

Some of us are just like that now, and we call ourselves blessed and highly favored. But as soon as opportunity possesses something we jump head first into it. In this season I am praying for a genuine conviction to set in the hearts of God's people. Many of us are walking around here as the 'walking dead" and don't even realize it, and true enough we are all tempted, but it's the willpower that we all should have that keeps us from giving in. so we have different groups of people

1. They don't know any better

2. They just don't care

3. And you have the "I'm-a-saved Christian-I-can-do-what-I-want-and-ask-for-forgiveness-afterwards."

Now what I mean by those that don't know any better are those people who may have some mental defect about

Confessions of a Preacher's Daughter

them that affects their thinking. And the select few boundaries that God's word has not reached. Not my sister or brother that says "I wasn't raised in the church." well my friend after you got grown and on your own, it then became your choice to get to know God. It wasn't mamma and daddy fault. IT IS YOUR FAULT!

So! Now you have the," just don't care" bunch, the ones who say they don't care about life or they are just living it up, most people like this don't believe in God, heaven, and hell. So they live their lives to the fullest in complete sin. And most of the time if you ask them "why did you do this and that," their answer will be: AND... SO WHAT! WHO CARES?"

Now, to the I'm-a-saved Christian-I can-do-what-I-want-and-ask-for-forgiveness-afterwards, almost half of the Christians I come in contact with have this mindset. They live their lives thinking they will die at a ripe old age, and then they will ask for their salvation on their deathbed. They believe they can do whatever, and when done they will fall on their knees and ask God to forgive them. SMH! I used to think this way, and it was my stupidity to the word that I felt this way.

True enough, God's grace and mercy, never ends. BECAUSE he allows us to awaken to each day, open our eyes, and allow us to see a whole day through to the next. For example, when I got shot in my shoulder back in 2007 outside the club, I knew better than to be there. Without a shadow of a doubt, I knew it was God's mercy that kept me from bleeding to death while I lay unconscious on the side of the building. He didn't have to do it, but he did. Another person was shot in the belly that night and died.

CHAPTER FOURTEEN—Temptations

Now, say I died, and the other person survived. Think about it. I knew better than to be at the club, and I was proclaiming to be a born-again Christian. I was not even trying to do the work God called me to do, but I was out drinking and clubbing. We don't know our own time on this earth, and that's why we should live every day in the fullness of God.

His word states: 1st Peter 4:1 NKJV

17}For the time has come for judgment to begin at the house of God; and if it begins with us first, what will be the end of those who do not obey the gospel of God? 18) Now, if the righteous one is scarcely saved, where will the ungodly, and the sinner appear?" 19) Therefore let those who suffer according to the will of God commit their souls to Him in doing good, as to a faithful Creator.

We as the saints are barely getting into heaven, and we will make our paths to get there even harder if we continue to live anyway and living in sin. I have seen many peers be taken out right in their mess. There was no time for them to call on God. I am so thankful that I was not that person on my way to hell the night I got shot. People you can't keep on living in sin and think you have all the time in the world to change your life because each of us has our, and we need to start focusing on what God has called us to do and living for him and not ourselves. So, first make up in your mind that you are ready for change and to live for God. Then ask him to deliver you from whatever it is that will keep you from your salvation, remember;

For the wages of sin is death, but the gift of God is eternal life through Jesus Christ our Lord.
Romans 6-23 KJV

Confessions of a Preacher's Daughter

I can speak on this because of where I come from because I was that person who would say, "I will ask for forgiveness." I would club, drink, smoke, curse, shack up, and be promiscuous. I did it all, and I am so thankful that true conviction set in, and I received true deliverance. So, people let's get saved for real and turn away from temptations and sin!

CHAPTER FIFTEEN

HELP OR NO HELP

CHAPTER FIFTEEN—Help or No Help

Sometimes I wonder what goes on in the minds of the molester. We all try to make up excuses for our sins. However, do we give those in the church the same grace we desire? Do we grant a slap on the wrist for lusting after the little girls and boys in the church and say, "Oh they know better. We just gon' pray for their healing of this," or do we get them the help they need? Do we throw away the key and say, "To hell with them?" Hmmm?

Well, I think it starts with the molester. First of all, do they know they have a problem? Do they want to stop? Are they even trying to quit?

I was molested at the age of 9 up to 15 years old, by two different men. One a drummer in a gospel group and the other was a pastor. At the time I wasn't the only little girl these men were molesting. They also had wives and daughters of their own.

So, how do we know when it's all an act with the men in the church with high positions? Unless God gives you the spiritual eyes to see you won't know. My question to my readers is, How do we help someone who knows they have a problem but doesn't want to reform? How do you help or even recognize something is going on with the young girl or boy who has no voice or is too fearful to speak up?

Earlier in this book, I stated when we have these issues do we blame others, our parents, other adults that did the same thing to us when we were kids, do we blame generational curses, or do we blame that good old flesh of ours? I feel that when a person continues to do wrong, lusting after young girls, cheating on their wives, and saying I know I have a problem but won't stop, that's their flesh.

Confessions of a Preacher's Daughter

There is no excuse for sin. It's sad when the little girls come to you about a man in the church and tell you he's been trying to mess with her or her friends. Only to realize this same man been after you and other grown women in the church, and has a wife at home. One of my favorite sayings is, I will pray for and love you from a distance, but until you want help, you won't stop the sin.

CHAPTER SIXTEEN

WHAT DOES IT TAKE?

CHAPTER SIXTEEN—What Does It Take?

In today's world we define love as an emotion that we feel, but how do we show love? Is it in our actions, is it unspoken body language, or is it only shown through physical and sexual contact is it being financially stable, I believe that it is all the above, if you have one that's lacking then you may want to reevaluate the person who says they love you.

In many marriages, they lead to divorce because either you got the physical, sexual, and emotional part but it's lacking the stability of someone being responsible for one's self and family. And it always the one that is doing the lacking that seems to believe that they are not wrong, or sometimes it's they both are financially stable but lacking the physical, sexual, and emotional. So either way, you can't have one without the other. We push people to stay together because that's God's way, but sometimes we can lack the one thing he gave us which is common sense.

As Christians, we should push our brothers and sisters to stay in their marriages, but there is a limit to how far you push. I know from personal experiences that if you push a person too far, it can confuse them to a point until they may not be able to make their mind up and they will base decisions on what you or others want them to do. I have a motto and will stand by it, it's hard to give marital advice to any couple when you are not in-between the walls with that couple, it's good to share your personal experiences, but never tell a couple they have to, or they need to do this, because you are not there with them, you are only looking from the outside and, listening to what each individual has to say, but in many broken marriages each person, (wife or husband) is not going to tell you everything, so that's why we must only

Confessions of a Preacher's Daughter

tell couples to seek God in it, and let God lead you. Be a person who will pray for them that God's will be done.

Just as people use certain things in the bible and turn it around, we must not do this with marriage vows. Here something for you to think about, "WHAT GOD HAS PUT TOGETHER LET NO MAN PUT ASUNDER. " ok we as people sometimes don't wait on God so we put ourselves together and that's when we are out of the will of God. and then comes the hell that we could have avoided if we had waited on God. Secondly, "IN SICKNESS AND IN HEALTH, FOR RICHER OR POORER." You can disagree if you want but this is my personal view when both are doing what they supposed to do, not too many financial storms will come up. But if you are just plain out lazy and you are the cause of your storm, and you are doing nothing to make it leave, then you can't throw for richer or poorer up. If you are sick or disabled and it has caused you to lose your job then yes stick by each other that's something unfixable unless Gods changes your health.

Many people say you said your vows b4 God and the people, yes but God forgives and if your marriage fails don't think that he won't forgive you and want send who he has for you to you. This time you must honestly wait on him. Don't let people beat you down because of your marriage failing or if you left because your wife or husband was not doing what they supposed to do. Its ok to seek spiritual marriage guidance but always make your own choices because at the end of the day you are the one who has to go home with your spouse and only you and God know what's in your heart.

CHAPTER SIXTEEN—What Does It Take?

Do I speak off personal experiences? Yes, I do. Always use common sense, and it takes two doing everything it takes to keep a marriage together, just as it takes two to mess one up. Always seek God in what you should do. When you get your answer please my friend do what he says, because it could save your marriage, don't be slothful at all.

CHAPTER SEVENTEEN

PRESSURE

CHAPTER SEVENTEEN—Pressure

Many of God's people are experiencing the pressure of life, and it seems to be weighing them down. To some, it may seem very unbearable. To others, we try to avoid it or sit and do nothing.

Let's start off by defining what the word **pressure** means below.

1. The process of pressing steadily.

2. Constant state of worry and urgency

3. Forces that pushes or urges

· the applying of a firm regular weight or force against somebody or something

· powerful and stressful demands on somebody's time, attention, and energy, or demand of this sort· something that affects thoughts and behavior in a powerful way, usually in the form of several outside influences working together persuasively.

I want to encourage first myself and to anyone reading this that we must not give in to the enemy. As Luke 22:31 states, **"And the Lord said, Simon, Simon, behold, Satan has desired to have you, that he may sift you as wheat."** The devil has magnified our problems so big that we feel as though we can't handle them. He has taken the very test that God is putting us through or the wilderness experience we are in, and he is trying to use it to destroy us. He wants to get us to throw in the towel and give up right in the middle or for some you may be right at the brink of your blessing. Therefore, the enemy is working overtime to get you so off focus that you forfeit your blessing.

Confessions of a Preacher's Daughter

I can speak on this because of the place I am in right now. God never said life would always be peaches and cream. At times, I have felt like the pressures in my life have become too heavy for me to carry. When we start to think like this, the enemy will try to inflict all kinds of bad emotions upon us. With these emotions come different evil spirits that will try to attach themselves to us and try to keep us in dark places.

During the times when we feel like we can't stand the pressures, we must first keep our faith in God that he has not forgotten about us, and go through the process. Second, we must find ourselves fasting and praying until we see a change in our situation. Thirdly, we must arm ourselves with the full armor of God. "Therefore take unto you the whole armor of God, that you may be able to withstand in the evil day, and having done all, to stand. Ephesians 6:13

I want to encourage anyone who may be thinking of throwing in the towel spiritually or physically, not to do it. Remember, God has not forgotten about you, and the pressure you are feeling from your current circumstances are only tests of your faith, so please stand with me and go through it because on the other side is a great reward.

Jeremiah 29:11, "For I know the thoughts that I think toward you, says the LORD, thoughts of peace, and not of evil, to give you an expected end."

CHAPTER EIGHTEEN

TRYING TO OVERCOME IT ALL

CHAPTER EIGHTEEN—Trying to Overcome it All

We are hunted down but never abandoned by God. We get knocked down, but we are not destroyed. 2nd Corinthians 4:9 NLT

I want to encourage someone reading this to always be on guard and aware of the devil and his tricks. For so long, I would fall right into his traps, but God would turn right around and pull me out or spare my life. You can't tell me that God isn't a merciful God, because I am a living witness. I should have been dead a long time ago, but God didn't allow me to be taken out. Now, I knew the road ahead of me was going to be hard, because of how heavy the feelings were in me. To anyone reading this, don't make a decision based on what I've done or what you think I may have done. I put myself in most of the situations I found myself in, and then I went crying to God when he had already given me instructions on what to do. To those women who are single, wait on your God sent man. Proverbs 18:22 says, he that finds a wife finds a good thing, not she that finds a good man. We must first hide in Christ and wait on Him. When we rush, we tend to do things prematurely, and when we do this, it causes our marriages to have defects.

My suffering was good for me, for it taught me to pay attention to your decrees. Your instructions are more valuable to me than millions in gold and silver. You made me, and you created me. Now give me the sense to follow your commands may all who fear you find in me a cause for joy. For I have put my hope in your word. I know that your regulations are fair; you disciplined me because I needed it. Psalm 119:71-75

Don't build your relationships and marriages off of lies and deceit, because it will inevitably fall to the ground. Wait on instructions from God, and you will prevent a lot of hurt and confusion. I learned a lot in my first marriage. Therefore, I want to warn you that when you are in the state of mind where you don't want to listen and no one can change your mind, it is going to be hard to make anything work. When you find yourself in that state of mind, you may not be able to accept the help and advice of others. At this point, God is the only one who will be able to get through to you.

I had so many pushing me and telling me that this man was my promise, but I couldn't see past the fact that I married under false intentions. It was hard for me to ask God to give me the heart to love the man I chose to marry. It was very hard for me being in a household with a man with whom I was not in love. I was confused, and I didn't know if he was who God wanted me as my husband. My spiritual sister, brothers, and parents told me he was, but I wasn't trying to hear what they were saying.

My mind was clouded with so much confusion and self-hate that it was hard for me to make a decision that was going to benefit me spiritually or emotionally. My husband and I separated during this time. I started falling back into my old habits. I got so off focus that I left my church because I had got exposed, and it seemed like the whole church knew about my issues. I knew people were talking about me behind my back, and I felt as if I couldn't trust anyone including myself. I had fallen, and I felt like I wasn't going to get back up. I was embarrassed, and it seemed as if my church family didn't love me because they were talking about me behind my back. I allowed my flesh to take over my very thought patterns and decision making, which could have cost me my life, as well as my walk with God.

CHAPTER EIGHTEEN—Trying to Overcome it All

I decided to take a week vacation to Baltimore, MD, to visit some family and clear my mind. Once I came back, I went back to my church and apologized to my spiritual parents. I asked for restoration from God on Easter Sunday, and believe me it took every ounce of strength to walk up to the altar. Once I was there, I poured my heart out to God and repented. My marriage ended end in divorce, but I knew it was for the best because it was not what God wanted for me. Unknowingly, I would have to endure many more test and trails to see the results of what God wanted for my life.

Women, be careful when you jump and make a permanent decision for a temporary situation without listening to God. Somewhere in your future, you'll find yourself in a tough place or someone else's bed. Now, I'm not saying God won't work out decisions you have made, but if it's in his will, then you have to endure to the end to see results. You have to be led by God when faced with a life-changing decision. You may even have to take some time out for yourself, where it's just you and God, and analyze your priorities and your situation to find yourself. I had to stop and find myself again. Believe me, it's a process, and it's not going to happen overnight. I made some of the stupidest decisions during this period, and I got off track numerous times. I finally had to put my foot down and say to the devil, "You can't have me anymore!" I was at a point in life where I was saying, "Ok God, who am I and what is it that you have placed in me?" Well, that old devil did what he could do to try and keep me bound so that I wouldn't find out.

I had to draw closer to God because the enemy was stomping on my head, kicking me in my back, and screaming in my ears. I knew if I didn't set myself free I was going to die, spiritually. Once I got out there, the enemy would have taken me out physically, so that he could laugh in my face.

When you find yourself in a situation where you feel like throwing in the towel, do a self-check, ask God to forgive you, forgive yourself, and draw closer to God. Once you are there, fight to stay under his wing. Even if you are still just a teenager and you feel like there is no one on this earth you can go to who loves you, know that you have a Father in heaven you can go to about anything.

Find yourself a secret place and talk to him. There is no specific way to speak to God, just talk to him; he's waiting for you. Go to Him when you feel like you're falling victim to your flesh, and He will give you the strength you need. You can fast and pray at any age because He always answers, no matter your age. He is no respecter of person. Don't be the stubborn little girl I was because God may not give you as many chances as he gives someone else. God had every right to send me to an early grave. He gave me warning after warning, and most of the time I turned around and did things anyway, knowing I was disobeying him. We must not get so comfortable and think that we are going to die at an old age, because God could take us out right in our mess and send us to a burning hell. I realized that if I didn't get it together, I was headed for destruction. Don't be tricked into falling back into old ways and picking up old habits of getting what you want and need, because when you do this, you are letting your flesh take control and are not being led by God. When we don't allow God to guide us, it only makes our process harder.

Many sorrows come to the wicked, but unfailing love surrounds those who trust in the Lord.
Psalm 32:10 NLT

CHAPTER EIGHTEEN—Trying to Overcome it All

You have to seek counsel from God. Sometimes we have to isolate ourselves to see ourselves for who we are. I did endure a lot of pain and had a lot of decisions to make, but in the process when I found myself at my lowest point, I couldn't call on anyone but God. Until then, I ran in circles and hit the wall every time. I ran from God and disobeyed him over and over again. Each time I always fell into the devil's tricks and traps. When you keep on doing that, there will come a time when He's going to draw back His hand from you. When that happens, His wrath will fall upon you. No one wants the wrath of God to fall upon them. He will cause exposure, and you may even get taken out physically without the chance to say, "Lord, here I am. Save me. I repent." God is not a God to play with because when you do, you are playing on very dangerous grounds.

Even though I knew as a young woman that God had a great work for me to do, I didn't want to step into it, and that voice in my head told me that it wasn't so. There was night during Bible Study when the Prophetess spoke to me and let me know that I would teach and speak too many, that was my confirmation of what I already knew that God had placed in me. For so long the voices in my head told me that I was too shy, my speech wasn't good enough, no one will read or buy my book, but this was the same voice that the Minister at the Women's Conference told me that was assigned to me as a child to torment me in my mind. The enemy will play with your mind until you don't know who is talking to you. Therefore, we must arm ourselves daily as Ephesians 6:10-20 teaches.

We also have to keep the ones that mean us no good from speaking in our ears so much to the point that we can't hear God. You may think it's God talking, but when you step back and let God handle the situation, you will then see who was actually talking. So many young women and men never open themselves up to God, and they stay bound all the way to their grave. God loves all of us, we are his creation, and we are wonderfully made in his image. As the scripture says, seek ye first the kingdom of God above all else (Matthew 6:33). When we put God first above all others and the things of the world, He will bless in ways we never dreamed. So don't think that God has forgotten about you, or that you are unworthy of eternal life. God already knew what you were going to go through because it was all designed for you to be blessed.

If you are going through and having problems remember, problems come from:
1. **Self-Induced Disobedience**
2. **God Himself, as a test**
3. **The devil**
4. **Lack of Knowledge**

So be on guard of the enemy and stand firm. If he can keep you out, he will keep you weak. God doesn't always show us the big picture, but He will give us a glimpse so that we can push through our obstacles. Stop focusing on the problem because when you do this, it will only get you down. In Ecclesiastes 9:12, it tells us that we never know when some things are going to put us in a hard place, and that we are always caught by certain tragedy, meaning we can't predict when hard times are coming, so we must not become unstable in mind to where we can't hear God. We must also be careful not to blame God when bad things do happen in our lives. God may have taken his hands off you to show you that you need Him, so stop doubting Him when he has already gone before you.

CHAPTER EIGHTEEN—Trying to Overcome it All

But I say unto you, don't be shocked or afraid of them. The Lord your God is going ahead of you. He will fight for you, just as you saw him do in Egypt.
Deuteronomy 1:29-30 NLT

If you carefully obey all the commands I am giving you today, and if you love the Lord your God and serve him with all your heart and soul, then he will send the rains in their proper seasons-the early and the late rains-so you can bring in your harvest of grain, new wine, and olive oil. He will give you lush pasture land for your livestock, and you yourselves will have all you want to eat.
Deuteronomy 11:13-15 NLT

Many of you may wonder why I am sharing my story, but I pray that this touches someone's heart and helps someone who is going through similar situations. Don't make the same mistakes I made. Many of them were from a lack of knowledge, and some were self-induced by disobedience. I started having sex at an early age. When young women do this, it gets very addicting to the point that we have a hard time trying to stop. So, when you find yourself curious about sex, stop and ask yourself, "Is he or she worth it?" If I could go back and change some things my life would be different.

I want to encourage you to hide yourself in God, at an early age, and let him lead you in every decision. I'm not saying the process will be easy, but when you start to feel a little weak call on God. Don't do as I did by fighting God. I challenged his ways continually, and each time he whipped me. I always got exposed when I was doing something, no matter how hard I tried to hide it. Even when I knew it was wrong, I would still do it because I was letting my flesh take

Confessions of a Preacher's Daughter

over my thinking and how I did things. In the end, I was always right back in God's face crying and begging him to take away the burden I had put on myself.

God gives us many chances, but many people go to their grave because they won't listen to Him and continue to run from him. God is a jealous God, and when we start putting this world and man before Him, His wrath will inevitably fall upon us. I knew there was greatness upon my life, but I let the enemy trick me over and over again, by giving him room to make me believe that I was nothing. When we do this, we set ourselves back spiritually, and when we try to birth something, it comes out handicapped, because we doubt the gifts He has placed on the inside of us.

God gives you many gifts when you come into the world from your mother's womb. Many people walking this earth are anointed and don't even realize it. They are running from their anointing, don't believe it, or they haven't stepped into the knowledge of the Word and God. Everyone goes through different experiences in life. If some of us would tell our stories, we never know who we could help or prevent from making the same decisions. I know this is not your average story or inspirational book, but my prayer is that I help someone get on the right track and fight to stay on it. My story doesn't end here, and I know there will be many more trials and tests to come.

As some of you may have read in my previous book, **Keeping the Faith While Saying Goodbye**, we must keep our faith in God that He will see us through it all.

The first step to deliverance is to admit it. Many people looked at me as the preacher's daughter and wondered why I turned out as I did. Well, my answer to that question is that each of us is on a life path. Some of us took wrong turns

CHAPTER EIGHTEEN—Trying to Overcome it All

and strayed off the track. Once I did get back on the right road, my journey was still like no one else's.

Your breaking always comes before your blessing. Sometimes we go through much pain and hurt, some of which we brought on ourselves, but trust that God will heal and deliver all if we give it to Him and have the faith that He will do as he promised. I thank God for not letting me die in my mess. God chastens those He loves. We are all on the same path, but each journey is different. So be careful in the decisions you make. May God bless you and keep you.

EPILOGUE

EPILOGUE

EPILOGUE

I decided it was time for me to move out of the state. In my mind, to get a new start in life and felt it was doable by putting myself in a different atmosphere. So, I moved to a city about an hour and a half away from Dallas. After being there a few months, I finally got the chance to meet my biological family on my father's side. I met two of my aunts, my grandmother, and a sister I never knew I had. However, I still did not meet my biological father. Apparently, he had not been a father to her either. We have all kept in contact since then. I thank God for making it possible to connect with them after not knowing them for over 30 years.

WHEN YOU LEAST EXPECT IT

Out the blue on Christmas Morning 2016, I received a Facebook video call from my biological father; a man I had never met or seen in my life. Talk about a surprise! Only God knows what the future holds with that chapter that is yet to be written.

You will find more of my story concerning the loss of my first two (2) stillborn sons in my book, **Keeping the Faith while Saying Goodbye.**

This Good News tells us how God makes us right in his sight. This is accomplished from start to finish by faith. As the scripture says, *it is through faith that a righteous person has life.* (Romans 1:17 (NLT)

In Memory of my brother, Garry, my niece Christiana, and my sons, Jeremiah, Avery, Josiah & Aaron

POEMS

POEMS BY TAMEKA

LIFE

Life is like a leaf falling in the air

You don't know where it will land

Life is so much like this leaf

For in life we find ourselves

In many situations and don't know where they will lead us to

So to get the leaf to go where you want it

You must blow it

In the direction you want it to go

We must apply this to our lives

Hard Love

Love can be hard to deal with

Sometimes it can bring confusion

It'll bring you down to tears

It seems as though the person you love the most is who hurts you the most no matter what they do, you still love them

That's where you have to be strong, and learn to handle the love you share

We all learn from our mistakes, and when we do that, if two people were meant to be, they'll learn from their mistakes and move on

POEMS BY TAMEKA

DAYDREAMING

Why does it hurt so bad?
Sitting here daydreaming
and fantasizing of things never to come
Things just not right, I don't understand
All I ask for is to be loved and understood
Still waiting on that angel to fall from the sky
But in vain, it seems as if he'll never come
It's a shame to be alone,
and to hurt as bad as I do
I give my love and it always gets abused
Is happiness not for me?
Will I live alone the rest of my life?
Will I die an unhappy woman?
Now I know why, "the caged bird sings".
She sings to be free to fly as a free spirit
I too want to be free
Free from all this hurt, pain, and anger
No one knows my pain,
No one can go where I've been
So I will continue to wait on that angel to fall
from heaven.

Confessions of a Preacher's Daughter

The Mirror

*There's a mirror, let me take a look in it.
Come take a look in it if you like.
Hmm....what do you see?
Do you like what you see?
I know what I see when I look, but it puzzles me that you don't see what I see.
You say you see me as a stuck up woman, think she better that everybody else, or how someone put it, "church girl", other say she's weak minded and she'll never get it.
Hmm, you know I'm still confused, because that not what I see.
Maybe you need to take the shades off your eyes and put some 3d glasses on because it seems as though you can't see too well.
You call me strange, different, and crazy.
But you know it's funny to me that you're talking about what I look like, but can't seem to see what you in your reflection.
You know it's not my place to tell you what u look like when u should see it for you self.*

*But what I see in mines is change,
new creature, God's child*

POEMS BY TAMEKA

Oh what a wonderful person
God has made me to be,
But you still have the nerve to call me ugly.
So maybe you need to turn the light on or get a brighter light because I see a saved and filled with the Holy Spirit woman.
Please tell me how you can say anything about my reflection when your vision is obstructed from your own.
You need to clean up some things so that you can see clearly, because I believe you are all mixed up.
The reflection you claim to be mines.
Hmm... look a little harder.. Familiar isn't it,
It's not me, but you.
But you know, you can't be because, if you tried to look like me you couldn't even fit the shoes, so the next time you start to talk about some else's reflection, stop and take a look in the mirror

Confessions of a Preacher's Daughter

Can You Love A Woman Like Me?

Love me for me.
Love the God in me.
Love me for my personality.
Love me for my unfailing heart.
Love me for the mother that I am to my children.
Love me for my ideas.
Love the strong woman in me.
Love me for my gifts.
Yeah it's good to like my looks.
Yeah it's good to like me as mate.
But don't love me for my body.
Don't love me for sex.
The bible says he that finds a wife finds a good thing and is highly favored with God!
I am that virtuous proverbs 31 woman.
Yes I am different from other women.
That is what makes me unique.
Don't waste your time trying to understand me.
Who can truly love a woman like me?
I am unique.
Don't try to understand me.
You'll waste a lifetime trying.
There will never be another like me.
I am different, so I have been told.

POEMS BY TAMEKA

My personality is rare and confusing to some.
I am a beautiful strong black woman.
I am easy to love.
And when I love, I love from the depths of my soul.
I speak my mind boldly, and don't bite my tongue just to hold the truth.
I do what it takes to survive.
My kid want for nothing, God had blessed me with enough, because I am not full of greed.
Look into my eyes and you will find a deep mystery, which will leave you wanting to look deeper.
Hmm...Can you handle a woman like me?

Confessions of a Preacher's Daughter

Alzheimer's

Who am I?
I don't know the person in this mirror.
She's old and wrinkled.
That couldn't be me.
I'm young and beautiful.
Who am I?
I move around slow.
I can't see well.
I don't need a diaper!
Where are all my teeth?
Why do I need this walker?
I can walk just fine.
I'm afraid, please don't leave me alone.
I don't understand?
Who is this woman looking back at me in the mirror?
That can't be me.
Someone please take me home.
How did get to this place?
Where is my husband? We just got married.
I'm not 75 years old!
Shut up! I'm not that woman in the mirror.
Help me please!
Who am I?

POEMS BY TAMEKA

ENTER INTO THE MIND OF ME, THE BLACK WOMAN

What does the world see when I walk I the room?

A weaker vessel to the man because I am woman, oh! And did I mention I am a black woman? Before you even get to know me, you have already made up in your mind that I am a good for nothing, loud, uneducated, ratchet black woman.

Tell me how many people of all races run to all the hand-outs the government offers, but because I am black, I am labeled as a black woman who wants a hand out, when in actuality I am a second class income class of making too much to get any assistance from our government.

I get turned down for jobs because I refuse to put chemicals in my hair as society has fooled my people into thinking it's a curse to wear our hair in its natural state. I cannot not change the fact that God put into my DNA for my hair to grow as wool or cotton in an upward position and not as fine silk in a downward position as society would prefer it be. Or I cannot wear my hair in braids, or cornrows, or my hair is too big

Confessions of a Preacher's Daughter

because of its length and thickness. No matter what way I wear my hair, it's going to be unprofessional if I just come to work with it in a ponytail, or as you say ghetto, and ratchet styles, so what do you want me to do? Shave it all off?

So you the good old United States who sells those lies of the so called American Dream to foreigners, you say come here it's so wonderful to live here. I could make millions but still looked down on because I am a woman who happens to be black. How about my sister over here who is a shade darker than me who goes into Corporate America for a job, and they turn her away, and before she can get out the door good, You CEO's laugh among yourselves and say, "My, look how black and nappy headed she is. She will bring a negative look to our company." Not knowing that the woman who just walked out of your office was the one that could have brought your company billions of dollars.

The few white friends I have, when I am invited to their house, you look and think, "look there is a black person here, wonder why she is here and who invited her?".

My daughter once told me upon meeting her white friend's parents that, they don't associ-

POEMS BY TAMEKA

ate close with black people or have them in their home because of their view of all black people are the same. So before you even get to know me you have already labeled me.

But, yet I sat at a table and full of white parents, parents who our children play and hang out together, watching how deep in their conversation, purposely avoiding talking to me., while you sneak a glance at me from time to time, and when it's time to leave, I get asked, oh now whose parent are you again. Remember I was the only black person at the table. Need I say more?

Yes, my people get into trouble, yes my people kill others as well as each other, yes my people have some racists among them, yes my people seek and some will use the system, yes my people have a lot of single mothers. But doesn't your people also do and have the same issues as my people. Black on black crime white on white, Hispanic on Hispanic. But everyone is quick to say, look they kill they own kind, so why don't they just shut up. #BlackLivesMatter, The last time I checked all races kill their own. But this thing right here is how the black community is still treated and profiled. Yes, we have criminals but don't treat them worse than you would treat a white criminal who done the same crime.

  This thing is way deeper than just cop on black person crime, its legalized racism, I am already profiled when I step out in public.

  When will the judging of being black stop? Why are you afraid of me, when I have never shown myself violent to you? Why are you embarrassed to have me around your other friends and family? Why did you ask me how am I going to wear my hair before coming to your family picnic? Why? That answer, I guess would be," never", not until this world as we know it ends.

Confessions of a PREACHER'S DAUGHTER

BY TAMEKA LOVETT

My Prayer For You

Lord, I thank you for allowing me and giving me the strength to share my story and my heart with the world. Because without your guidance I wouldn't be able to tell my story. I pray that this book blesses every reader and that it helps some young man or woman in their daily struggles with life. May the reader know that it doesn't matter what they have done in their life. Let them know that you are always there and will never turn your back on them. Let them know that you are God and you will never forsake them. For you say, "Behold, I stand at the door and knock. If any man hears my voice and opens the door, I will come in, to him, and will sup with him and he with me." I pray the reader gains strength from me in knowing that hope and deliverance are in you. Thank you, Lord, Amen.

Tameka S. Lovett

Tameka Shanta Lovett is the author of acclaimed book, *Keeping the Faith While Saying Goodbye*. She is an advocate for women and families who have *angel babies*. In her second release with College Boy Publishing, she delves deep into her childhood and past, in an attempt to heal from the years of hurt, molestation, abuse, and neglect. Lovett currently resides in Dallas Fort Worth area, works as a medical technician and freelance photographer.

Keeping the Faith While Saying Goodbye

Paperback: 96 pages
Publisher: College Boy Publishing (January 19, 2016)
Language: English
ISBN-10: 1944110194
ISBN-13: 978-1944110192
EBook ISBN 13: 978-1-944110-20-8

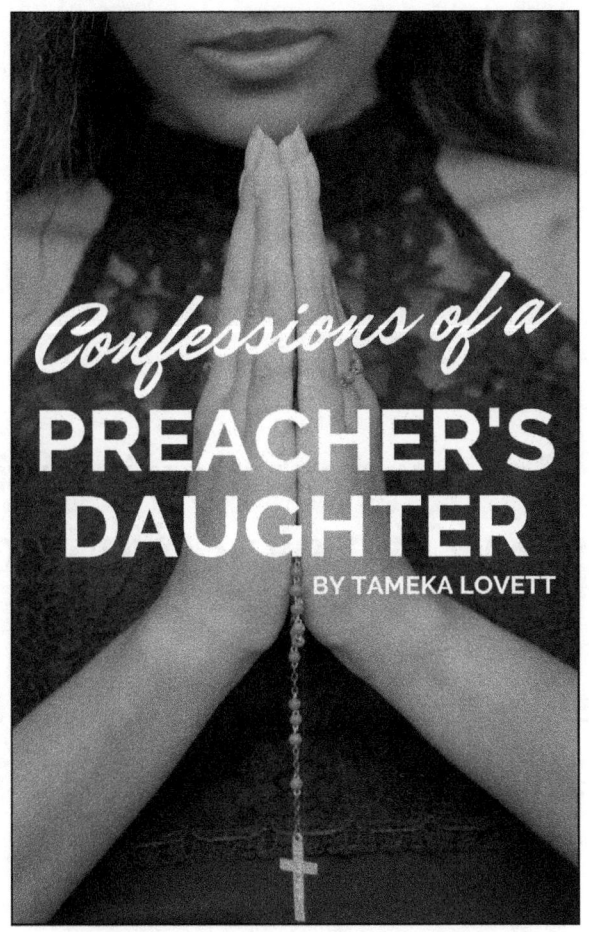

Confessions of a Preacher's Daughter

Paperback: 168 pages
Publisher: College Boy Publishing (January 29, 2018)
Language: English
ISBN-10: 1-944110-43-7
ISBN-13: 978-1-944110-43-7
EBook ISBN13: 978-1-944110-44-4

For autographed copies visit:
www.TamekaLovett.com

Tameka Lovett is available for book signings, media interviews, ministry, and conferences.

www.ingramcontent.com/pod-product-compliance
Lightning Source LLC
Chambersburg PA
CBHW071608170426
43196CB00034B/2228